This book has been p
0949-19000 PC.

All rights are reserved by the author. This book may not be reproduced in any form.

Copies of this book can be obtained from the author at:

    James Lewis
    19713 32nd Ave.
    Conklin, MI 49403

Unless scripture is cited within the context of a quotation from another source, scripture quotations are either from (ESV) English Standard Version, or (NIV) New International Version.

Cover by Jason Blackburn

Thank you for supporting this ministry
Jim

Table of Contents

Foreword

Acknowledgements

Preface

Introduction

Chapter One – Caring/Sharing
- Robert Chapman
- Mother Teresa
- George Washington Carver
- JoAnn Cayce
- Daniel Cayce
- Parker Ceplina
- Ranya Kelly

Chapter Two – Selflessness
- John Fling
- Lori Lewis
- Mick Doane
- Dave Irwin
- Albert Mansor
- Sarah Six

Chapter Three – Discipleship
- Zach Bonner
- Billy Graham
- Bishop Fulton J. Sheen
- Bill Gaither
- Nick Vujicic
- David Wilkerson

Chapter Four – Sacrifice/Trust
Todd Beamer

Nate Saint, Jim Elliott, Ed McCully, Pete Fleming, Roger Youderian, Rachel Saint, Elisabeth Elliott
Alvin York

Chapter Five – Integrity/Character
Samuel Adams
Dan Quayle
Sarah Palin
Mike Huckabee
John McCain
Ernie Harwell
Roberto de Vincenzo
Ronald Reagan

Chapter Six – Courage of Conviction/Covenant
Lance Sijan
Kirk Cameron
Craig and Mark Keilburger
Tim Tebow, Pam Tebow
Hermine (Miep) Gies

Chapter Seven – Compassion/Mercy
Dr. Ben Carson
Dr. Dale A. Matthews
Jamie Balcom
Millard and Linda Fuller
Sean and Leigh Anne Tuohy
Beth Anthony

Chapter Eight – Repentant
Pat Boone
Lee Strobel
Chuck Colson
George Foreman

Chapter Nine – Inspire Others
Red Skelton
Mr. T (Laurence Tureaud)

Audie Murphy
Joe Foss
Joshua Chamberlain
Dan Kirchgesler
Unknown Song Be, Vietnam village leader
Ty Pennington
Truett Cathy
Dave Dravecky
Payne Stewart

References

Foreword

It is one thing when you use the word "invisible" within the title of a book, but add the word "heroes" and it becomes another thing altogether.

Jim has taken what, for some, might be the mundane and wrapped stories of honor and integrity, love and strength in a book that is a reflection of your neighbor. We all are called to make a difference in the lives of others - not just for the purpose of satisfying our own agenda, but for the greater good; the invisible heroes brought to light within these pages are a reflection of what is possible in all of us. Each tale is a measure against how we live our lives in a world filled with chaos, through grace.

As I think of Jim's intent and how each page builds upon the last, this book, with its grounding in scripture, easily lends itself as a notable tool for Bible study, as well as finding a place in family reading. The power of what the reader will enjoy is the personal touch which draws each of us to lives touched by the hero. These heroes show us how to be what we are called to be as members of the human race and, moreover, how to be living examples of Christ. The heroes make a difference, not for their own sake, but rather for the interaction that plays out in their lives.

The interactions are all but invisible to the greater population of the world, but each marks a place within society for the better good. Each might say it is just a normal example of how they are, or that it's no big deal, but for the few that bear witness to the events of their lives, they are held in awe. It is an awe that draws us closer to the "why." Why, because of the steps taken which align them and us to the Cross. Why, because we need heroes that are not plagued by society's call for over-indulgence. Why, because we need to see Christ in action through one another.

Thank you, Jim for your willingness to be an expression for these invisible heroes.

Reverend Tony De La Rosa
Conklin Reformed Church

Acknowledgement

I am humbled and thankful that Jesus paid for my sins with His life so I have the opportunity to share a place at His table. All I have to do is acknowledge Him as my Savior, ask Him to come into my life, and then proclaim His word to those who may not know of Him, which He has blessed me with the ability, talent, and passion to do through this book. If you don't have a personal relationship with Him yet, delve into His Word and seek an understanding of His love and grace through fellowship with the body of Christ – His church.

There are many people who helped in the production of this book. I want to especially thank my wife, Pat, for her patience in proofreading and correcting all of my embarrassing errors and omissions. I am also grateful to those who scrutinized the manuscript for theological content. Their candid assessment helps ensure that I am not leading anyone in any direction but toward God.

I also want to thank all of the invisible heroes who have come along side me through my journey to the Cross and who continue to help me stay the course and run the good race. Please remember that Jesus is the example we are to follow.

Thank you for sharing in my mission through the purchase of this book. Please keep our church family in your prayers as we reach out to our community and share God's love as invisible heroes to the people around us.

Preface

Other books have focused on select attributes of a person's life that reflect Christ, but not on how the person mirroring the attribute lived out his or her life. Selectively focusing on single attributes provides limited comparison of our lives to the One True example, and gives us a false sense of security in our righteousness - right standing with God. He doesn't want us to turn over just a part of our lives to Him; He wants us to give Him our all. I have made every effort to exercise due diligence in selecting people to profile who reflect the single standard that we should be comparing our lives to – Jesus Christ.

I cannot overemphasize the purpose for this book. It is about attributes, not the people I chose to profile. The people profiled are not to be held up as idols for they are simply an instrument God uses to demonstrate the way we should live our life for Him. I also do not want to imply that any of the people I selected are without sin, for we have all fallen short. A recent article in *Have a Good Day* put our relationship with God and His expectations of us in a perspective that matches my intent for this book. The author of the article states,

> Realizing just how inadequate we are is the first step in getting right with God. Only the person who has made an honest appraisal of him- or herself and recognized his or her sins will seek God's pardon. And God 'will not reject a broken and repentant heart' (Psalm 51:17). Forgiveness and salvation are for those who recognize that they don't measure up.
>
> You only need to acknowledge your sins, turn to God, and by faith acknowledge Jesus Christ as your Savior. When you do, you'll receive 'the right to become children of God' (John 1:12), with eternal life as your inheritance.

Part of my focus is on good works that people have done for others during their journey to the Cross. However, that should not be interpreted as the way to achieve God's grace. In Ephesians 2:8-9 (ESV) Paul tells us, "For by grace you have been saved through faith. And this is not your own doing; it is the gift of God, not a result of works, so that no one may boast." Instead of relying on works to achieve God's grace, Paul later states, "Therefore be imitators of God, as beloved children. And walk in love, as Christ loved us and gave himself up for us, a fragrant offering as sacrifice to God" (Eph 5:1-2 ESV).

Obedience to God will naturally lead to good works that emulate God's love, which is what is really being profiled. Isaiah said, "Is it not to share your food with the hungry and to provide the poor wanderer with shelter – when you see the naked, to clothe him, and not to turn away from your own flesh and blood? Then your light will break forth like the dawn, and your healing will quickly appear; then your righteousness will go before you, and the glory of the Lord will be your rear guard. Then you will call, and the Lord will answer: you will cry for help, and he will say: Here am I" (Isa 58:7-9a).

God has a plan for each of us, but he also allows us to make choices. Some of our choices lead us toward God, and some lead us away. Remaining in the choices that lead us away from God, and possibly causing others to follow our direction was a concern that was always on my mind during my time of research and writing. I have tried to continually be aware that God knows where my heart is. I ask for your prayers that my work is from God and will be a blessing to Him.

As I mention in the introduction, it is not my goal to define who is righteous and who is not. Please pray that you will consider the entire word of God in your journey to the Cross, and not rely only on the message of well-intentioned authors, even one such as me.

There may be some controversy whether some of the people I profile in this book acknowledge Jesus Christ as their Savior, but I don't believe that there can be any argument that God is, or was, central in their life.

If, after reading this book, you still need more examples to follow, I suggest you open your Bible to almost any page and begin reading with conviction. If you want specific examples, read about Paul, Timothy, Titus, Peter, John, and James. Paul used himself as an example to the people of the Church of Philippi when he said, "What you have learned and received and heard and seen in me – practice these things, and the God of peace will be with you"

(Php.4:9 ESV). May you always be mindful that others learn, hear, see, and receive from you also.

Introduction

Become, "A voice of one calling in the desert,
'Prepare the way for the Lord, make straight paths for him.'"
-Matthew 3:3 (NIV)

You might wonder if the title I have chosen is referring to one book or two. The main title, Invisible Heroes, could probably be developed on its own as could the tag line, footsteps to the Cross. But I felt compelled to blend them together to achieve a perspective of "hero worshiping" that is too often missing from the criteria we generally use to determine who we want to fashion our life after or who we want to emulate.

This book is a compilation of stories of famous and not-so-famous people. Whether a person achieved the name recognition status of someone we would consider "famous" was not criteria for their inclusion in the following pages. There will undoubtedly be some familiar names, but there will also be names of people known only to me or a small circle of that person's friends. As you read the profiles of the latter group feel free to substitute people from your own circle of relationships when their attributes align with the person I've chosen.

The invisible side of this book brings into account the people around us who go about their lives without fanfare or desire to be in the spotlight. The person could be a pastor, neighbor, colleague at work, local celebrity, teacher, neighborhood grocer, or even a family member. All too often we fail to recognize the people we should really be emulating and instead focus on people with lots of money, name recognition, political status or some other characteristic, positive or negative, that makes them newsworthy. Such a narrow view creates a perception that we should aspire to model our life to reflect that person's character. What I found during my research for this book is that sometimes a person's character is only skin deep. I was very disappointed to find that some of the people I held in high regard had the skin of a hero, but inside they were troubled and confused about what really matters.

Who am I to judge whether a person is a hero or not? It is not my intention to pass judgment on any person, whether they are included or excluded from this book. The intention is to profile individuals who display values that reflect how God expects us to live our life for Him. The only authoritative basis I used for determining who would be included in this work is *my* interpretation – flawed as that might be - of God's Word - the Bible. The Bible gives us many clues and directions for living a life worth emulating. I will reference some of them throughout the book, but my list is not intended to be all inclusive. The most important thing for all of us to remember is that if we focus on Jesus we will never go wrong. His footsteps are hard to walk in, so it's gratifying to know that no matter where ours take us, He is always there to guide us back to His path.

That leads into the tag line, footsteps to the Cross. As I mentioned, it is not my intention to pass judgment. It is also not my intent to determine if a person is Christian or not. In fact, I profile a few people who come from a Jewish background. Others view faith as being very personal so they don't wear it on their sleeve for all to see. Does someone have to proclaim to be a Christian to lead another person to the Cross? I don't think so. I'm sure there are theologians who would label that statement as pure blasphemy. However, one of my heroes, my father, led me to the Cross while, unbeknownst to me, he was struggling with his own journey there. In his later years he confided that he hadn't accepted the Lord as his Savior until he was 46 years old. I was 20 at the time and looking back on our journey together I didn't see one point where he strayed from the path. I have to confess that my own journey took the same course and my timing for accepting Christ was exactly the same – when I was 46. I feel blessed that God was patient during my ignorance and that He allowed me time to recognize my errors. Now that my eyes and heart are open to Him, I recognize that He was always with me no matter how far I strayed from the path to the Cross. Even now I still consider my transformation to be a work in progress. God hasn't finished molding me yet.

Before getting too far along with my focus on the Cross, I should emphasize that the Cross does not save; Jesus saves. Even though we might follow someone's footsteps to the Cross, we still have to open our hearts, ask Jesus to come into our lives, accept His grace, and be washed in His cleansing blood. In Paul's first letter to

Timothy he says, "Here is a trustworthy saying that deserves full acceptance: Christ Jesus came into the world to save sinners – of whom I am the worst. But for that very reason I was shown mercy so that in me, the worst of sinners, Christ Jesus might display his unlimited patience as an example for those who would believe on him and receive eternal life" (1 Ti 1:15-16 NIV). I have chosen to emphasize the Cross in the tag line as a reminder of the price He paid for our sins.

I recently had the privilege to witness new invisible heroes emerging from our Church family when the Youth Group hosted a Sunday service. I was also greatly honored by a young man who assumed my name and characteristics for a role in the service. He said I represented the kind of Christian he hoped to be some day. If he only knew how I struggle each day to focus on Christ, but I guess most Christians probably feel the same way about their journey.

We all know that neither Abraham nor John the Baptist were Christian yet their example of passion and zeal for following God's Word and obeying his commandments can lead us to the Cross just as surely as if we were following Christ's own steps. There were many people who **literally** followed Christ to the Cross on that terrible day, beheld his suffering, and still refused to believe. As I mentioned earlier, my father's footsteps, like those of the heroes in this book, led me to the Cross, but, like all of us, I had to make my own decision to accept Christ when I got there.

We all know people who can talk the talk without being able to walk the talk. We may perceive a person to be walking the talk by their public expression of faith, yet they display an entirely different side of their life when in the shadows. We hear or read about people like that regularly. For example, there are priests who have strayed from their vows, high-profile church leaders who have allowed greed to dominate their lives, political leaders who have used their position to gain sexual or monetary favors, and even presidents who ask for the Lord's blessing upon their administration while cavorting with aides or promoting abortion, gay rights, and a homosexual agenda that are all abominations to our Lord. Christ said, "I tell you the truth, it is hard for a rich man to enter the kingdom of heaven. Again I tell you, it is easier for a camel to go through the eye of a needle than for a rich man to enter the kingdom of heaven" (Mt 19:23-24

NIV). Hearing about the decadent lives of some of the rich and famous around the world makes those words all so real. I'm thankful wealth is not one of the burdens I have to contend with.

I have made every effort to utilize a variety of research sources to qualify candidates for inclusion in this book. The absence of a person's story doesn't mean s/he is not worthy of a hero's position, it is more likely due to simple space constraints, or the absence of enough information sources. If you would like to recommend someone for future editions of this book, please pass them along. I will do my best to find a place of honor for them.

The attributes I use to determine a person's qualification as an invisible hero include, but are not necessarily limited to: 1. Selflessness instead of self-centeredness. 2. Sacrifice – giving up something for someone else. 3. Life reflecting Judeo/Christian values. 4. Integrity – being true to one's word. 5. Consciously pursuing a goal deemed unfavorable to one's career because it is the right thing to do. 6. Compassion. 7. Moral excellence and firmness. 8. Fallible, yet repentant. 9. Endeavoring to follow God's commandments. I have also included what Paul called the "fruit of the Spirit" in his letter to the people of Galatia, "But the fruit of the Spirit is love, joy, peace, patience, kindness, goodness, faithfulness, gentleness, and self-control" (Gal 5:22-23a NIV)

Commonly perceived attributes of a heroic individual that I didn't take into consideration are: extraordinary physical strength, extraordinary intelligence, extraordinary courage, or even extraordinary faith. Those are the attributes on the surface of a person's being that sometimes interfere with our ability to determine their true focus and whether their footsteps will lead us to the Cross.

I've heard reports indicating that as much as 70% of the population of the United States consider themselves to be Christian. If that were the case, writing this book would have been a simple task because 70% of the people I would have liked to profile would exhibit the characteristics of a hero whose footsteps would lead someone to the Cross. Unfortunately, my research didn't bear that out. Bible-exemplifying Christians are not the majority they are perceived to be. One only needs to examine his or her own priorities or those of people close to them to know that a person cannot profess to be Christian while supporting abortion, same-sex marriage, euthanasia, or political parties that espouse those agendas for their platform. This book is intended to enable the reader to examine how s/he should be living their beliefs so they will be the best example possible to those around them.

Are the eyes of your hero fixed upon Jesus? Can your hero lead you to the Cross? If you're not sure, I hope the following examples will help you see the invisible heroes that you should be fashioning your life after.

Parents, I encourage you to read this book through and examine your life and the people you emulate before passing it along to your children, but please do pass it along so they will have a model to follow as they attempt to walk in the…

Footsteps of Jesus

Lyrics: Mary B Slade   Composer: Asa B. Everett

Sweetly, Lord, have we heard Thee calling,
Come, follow Me!
And we see where Thy footprints falling
Lead us to Thee.

Footprints of Jesus,
That make the pathway glow;
We will follow the steps of Jesus
Where'er they go.

Though they lead o'er the cold, dark mountains,
Seeking His sheep;
Or along by Siloam's fountains,
Helping the weak.

Footprints of Jesus,
That make the pathway glow;
We will follow the steps of Jesus
Where'er they go.

If they lead through the temple holy,
Preaching the Word;
Or in homes of the poor and lowly,
Serving the Lord.

Footprints of Jesus,
That make the pathway glow;
We will follow the steps of Jesus
Where'er they go.

Then at last when on high He sees us,
Our journey done,
We will rest where the steps of Jesus
End at His throne.

Footprints of Jesus,
That make the pathway glow;
We will follow the steps of Jesus
Where'er they go.

Caring/Sharing

"Religion that God our Father accepts as pure and faultless
is this: to look after orphans and widows in their distress
and to keep oneself from being polluted by the world.
- James 1:27 (NIV)

As I mentioned in the introduction, Jesus said it was easier for a camel to fit through the eye of a needle than it was for a rich man to enter God's kingdom. I can't empathize with being rich, but I do wonder why it's so hard for people with material wealth to relate to those who have nothing. It seems that in order to relate, a person has to become like those s/he is trying to relate to. At least that is how it was for Robert Chapman when he made his decision to follow in Jesus' footsteps. Not much about Robert Chapman's life and work survived his death in 1902, but that didn't deter a tenacious author named Robert L. Peterson from chronicling his life in a biography published in 1995 by Loizeaux Brothers, Inc. of Neptune, NJ.

Robert Chapman was born in 1803 so you might wonder why I have included his profile with those of people of our time. He has been included as an example of the embodiment of selflessness, sacrifice, courage, compassion, and commitment that Jesus referred to in Matthew 19:16-21. Jesus told the rich man, "If you want to be perfect, go, sell your possessions and give to the poor, and you will have treasure in heaven. Then come, follow me."

Robert Chapman was born into a prominent family in Whitby, North Yorkshire, England. He was educated in the finest schools and became a prominent lawyer and a man of means in his own right. He attempted to follow God's call, but found he couldn't empathize with the people he was called to lead until he became like one of them. He gave away all of his possessions and claims to future inheritance, except for a small amount to purchase living quarters in the place God was directing him to.

Chapman received a calling to pastor at Ebenezer Chapel in Derby, an area we might refer to as a "suburb" of Barnstable, a coastal town southwest of London. He didn't hesitate to respond to the call. God was clearly in control of the opportunities available to Chapman in Derby. Peterson says, "The pockets of poverty reminded him of the London slums and his heart went out to their residents" (p. 45). However, ministering to the poor was not the only passion Chapman wanted to satisfy through the call to Derby. He heard about missionaries and preachers with no where to rest and recover from the labors of their work, so he determined to make a resting place for them. He felt if he could pray for them, talk to them, and encourage them they could return to their missions with renewed spirit.

Peterson wrote, "He found his ideal home in the Derby area. It was close to Ebenezer Chapel and it had room for guests" (p. 46). Chapman lived at his new residence, No. 6 New Buildings Street for seventy years. According to Peterson, "A friend once offered him the use of a large comfortable house in a better section of Barnstable, but Chapman declined. He wanted to live where even the poorest person could come to him without hesitation" (p. 46). Chapman appears to have been an incredibly visionary man. He understood that material wealth not only insulated people from the troubles around them, it also isolated them from opportunities to love one another and serve their fellow man.

As noted above, little of Chapman's writings survived him, but Peterson did find a note that expressed Chapman's view of how, "...one who is called to give himself entirely to the Lord's work holds a special place of responsibility" (P. 145). As Chapman put it:

> The Servant of the Lord Jesus must be instant in season and out of season, knowing that he is the Lord's messenger to every one with whom he has to do, and ever learning of the Lord; seeing that he is to be continually ministering to others, he must be receiving fresh supplies from the God of all grace through all channels. Meditation on the Word and prayer should aim at hearts and consciences, seeking in every way to magnify Christ and abase the creature. In short, he should set the Lord always before him, and so walk in His steps as to represent Him to every eye (P. 145).

Chapman was not alone in his perception of the responsibility of walking in Jesus steps. Mother Teresa viewed **her** ministry in the same way.

Agnes Gonxha Bojaxhiu, better known as Mother Teresa (1910 – 1997), wasn't born into a wealthy family like Robert Chapman, but she was by no means as poor as the people she cared for over more than 45 years in India and other areas of the World through her own order – The Missionaries of Charity. Like Chapman, Mother Teresa's early adult years were spent in relative solitude going through the motions of being a good Christian, but becoming anxious about not doing enough to share God's love, grace, and peace. After teaching in Calcutta for seventeen years, she felt compelled to respond to the suffering and poverty that surrounded her that her order was not able to minister to. When she left her order to follow her true calling, she, like Chapman, depended on Divine Providence to support her needs as she worked among the poorest of the poor in Calcutta. In her own words, Mother Teresa says that she served the poor because,

> I heard the call to give up all and follow Christ into the slums to serve Him among the poorest of the poor. It was an order. I was to leave the convent and help the poor while living among them (Callopy, 1996).

It wasn't possible for her to live in the simple comfort of the convent, free from the troubles that surrounded her. She couldn't be so close to the hunger without providing relief. She anguished over the absence of care for the victims of a society that shunned their collective responsibility to care for God's children, regardless of their social or religious status. From the same Website she said,

> When a poor person dies of hunger, it has not happened because God did not take care of him or her. It has happened because neither you nor I wanted to give that person what he or she needed. You and I, we are the Church, no? We have to share with our people. Suffering today is because

people are hoarding, not giving, not sharing. Jesus made it very clear. Whatever you do to the least of my brethren, you do it to me. Give a glass of water, you give it to me. Receive a little child, you receive me.

Her prayer for all of us was simply,
Make us worthy, Lord, to serve those people throughout the world who live and die in poverty and hunger. Give them through our hands, this day, their daily bread, and by our understanding love, give them peace and joy.

Mother Teresa received worldly fame and fortune during her lifetime, but she refused to accept any of it for her own use. When she won the Nobel Prize she turned over the cash portion of the award to her mission. The people she served needed the food, clothing, and medical supplies the award could purchase more than any comfort she needed from it.

It is hard to imagine being born into a more impoverished life than George Washington Carver (1864 – 1943) was. He didn't have to give up material wealth to empathize with the poor, he was one of them. However, he did forego material wealth and lavish offers from people like Henry Ford so he could stay focused on what really motivated him, caring for the lives and livelihood of poor Southern farmers.

George Washington Carver was motivated by only one thing, doing God's work. He felt that science was part of God's work, instead of two warring ideas. Although he is credited with a number of inventions, he applied for very few patents. He is reported to have stated that the ideas for the patented processes came from God, and he didn't have the right to sell them to anyone for profit. He willingly shared the testimony of his faith in Christ. After all, without Jesus as his foundation he would have been totally ineffective in science. His reliance on God to reveal scientific truth to him brought criticism from a number of his colleagues, but he found his strength in the fellowship of other Christians rather than in the scientific community.

If George Washington Carver hadn't been called to a life of science, a great number of people may have been left without any means of recovering from the devastation of their land by the farming practices of the day, not to mention the loss to future generations of scientists that studied under him and valued his work.

He truly believed that God created all men equal- and in His image. For him, that belief meant that racial and social barriers were nonexistent - at least in his classroom. His students learned a lot about character along with their academic studies. There are eight cardinal virtues at (George Washington Carver, 2010) that he expected his students to emulate and strive toward. They were:

- Be clean both inside and out.
- Neither look up to the rich nor down on the poor.
- Lose, if need be, without squealing.
- Win without bragging.
- Always be considerate of women, children, and older people.
- Be too brave to lie.
- Be too generous to cheat.
- Take your share of the world and let others take theirs.

George Washington Carver led a life for Christ on and off campus. I guess he could be called a 24/7 Christian. He led Bible classes for students at Tuskegee. He was very animated in his delivery of the Message and would often times act out the stories. Maybe that is why The Carver Academy blends academics, Judeo/Christian values, leadership, children's ministry opportunities, broadcasting, recording, and other activities in the learning environment they provide for grade school students. Try offering that in traditional secular schools. Carver's influence is still alive and well. God's work continues through his example.

I believe Robert Chapman, Mother Teresa, and George Washington Carver would be in complete agreement with an observation that Mother Teresa made concerning material wealth and how it encumbers a person's ability to truly see and empathize with the needs of others. She said, "The more you have, the more you are occupied, the less you give. But, the less you have the more free you are. Poverty for us is a freedom. It is not mortification, a penance. It is joyful freedom. There is no television here, no this, no that. But we are perfectly happy." Chapman recognized the wisdom in those words long before Mother Teresa uttered them. Chapman gave up all he had to minister to the poor and Mother Teresa gave up all she could have had. They both believed God's message through Jeremiah 7:23b, (NIV) "Obey me, and I will be your God and you will be my people. Walk in all the ways I command you, that it may go well with you."

I want to tell you about another Mother Teresa. This one happens to be a Baptist though. Her real name is JoAnn Cayce and she lives in Thornton, Arkansas. The local newspaper dubbed her the Mother Teresa of central Arkansas, but, like Mother Teresa, JoAnn doesn't like to be in the spotlight. Upon hearing she had been nominated for another award for her work she told Bill Halmandaris author of *Be the Light – A Blueprint for a Happy Life*, "I don't know what I've done that he (the mayor in a neighboring town) thinks is so special. I'm just doing what my mother and grandmother have done before me. And besides, I don't have much use for awards anyway. The president wanted to give me an award last year and I told him to put it in the mail" (p.28).

One of the awards that JoAnn has received is the Caring Award. The annual award is presented by the Caring Institute to people who honor and promote the values of caring, integrity, and public service. The award was inspired by the example of Mother Teresa. The citation for her award, which was presented in 1992, reads,

> Jo Ann Cayce, of Thornton, Arkansas, has worked tirelessly as a volunteer to relieve the suffering of the poor in South Arkansas. Cayce has spent her life bucking the bureaucracy, getting it to work for the people it's supposed to help but who have often

fallen through the cracks. She makes her rounds among the sick and diseased, battered women, and abused and neglected children. She fills out government papers and applies for assistance for the disabled and the mentally ill. She arranges for medical care for those who have no income or benefits to go to the doctor and provides them with transportation. She obtains appliances and housing for needy families and helps them pay utility bills. She helps people find job training and work. In addition, she writes hundreds of letters to legislators and local newspapers to advocate for the poor in our society. Cayce invites politicians and government officials to see the problems firsthand - to go with her to the homes of the poor, to the public health clinics and poverty-stricken schools. Cayce also collects gifts for area children who might not otherwise have a Christmas. She feeds hundreds at her Thanksgiving dinner and clothes thousands of adults and children with her clothing drives several times a year. She notes, 'For as long as I live and breathe I will be speaking out for the children and the poor in the hope that someday things will get better.' In doing so, Cayce performs miracles for those who would otherwise be forgotten.

This quote was included with her profile at the Caring Institute Website, www.caring-institute.org. It mirrors the view of the Lord's challenge to all of us. She said, "The best way in the world to forget your own troubles is to pick up somebody's load that's heavier than yours." It doesn't matter who you are and what condition your life is in, there is always someone who is carrying a heavier burden.

Halmandaris quotes her, "Everybody has got a purpose. Look at the poor. They make me feel needed. They have done for me more than I will ever do for them. They have given me purpose" (p. 29). What a remarkable philosophy, and it isn't lost on JoAnn alone. Caring and sharing continues to be the purpose for the Cayce family.

Her daughter Joannie and grandson Daniel are involved in the mission as well. In fact, Daniel has his own story.

Daniel started following his grandmother's example at the age of four. That is what I call following the footsteps of an invisible hero. Of course, JoAnn hasn't been invisible to Daniel. At the age of 16, Daniel also received the Caring Award and was inducted into the Caring Hall of Fame. His 2004 citation reads,

> Daniel Cayce's grandmother, Jo Ann Cayce, a 1992 Caring Awardee, is the founder of Jo Ann Cayce Charities, which for over half a century has often been the only salvation for the homeless and hungry in rural Arkansas. Daniel began initiating his own charitable projects in the winter of 1999-2000, when he gathered 300 blankets to distribute at one of his grandmother's food pantries. By the following winter, Daniel had collected over 1,200 blankets, 1,000 pots and pans, and 400 sets of boxed dishes. When he discovered that the WIC program excludes baby food, Daniel collected and distributed over 2,000 lbs. of baby food to poor families. 'I have always received motivation from my family to help those less fortunate,' says Daniel.

There is now an award named in honor of Daniel. The Daniel Cayce Award for Inspirational Leadership in Public Service is presented annually to an Arkansas High School student who has demonstrated outstanding service. Now there are people following the footsteps of young Daniel.

Another young man who is reaching out to meet the needs of others is Parker Ceplina of Michigan. Parker's ministry focuses on the elderly - specifically the residents of Brookcrest Retirement Community in Grandville, MI. Parker has been volunteering his time there since 2008 when he registered 388 hours of service to Brookcrest. In 2009 he volunteered more than 600 hours. Jesus told his disciples that when He comes again in His glory he will say,

> 'Come, you who are blessed by my Father, take your inheritance, the kingdom prepared for you since the creation of the world. For I was hungry and you gave me something to eat, I was thirsty and you gave me something to drink, I was a stranger and you invited me in, I needed clothes and you clothed me, I was sick and you looked after me, I was in prison and you came to visit me.'
>
> Then the righteous will answer him, 'Lord, when did we see you hungry and feed you, or thirsty and give you something to drink? When did we see you a stranger and invite you in, or needing clothes and clothe you? When did we see you sick or in prison and go to visit you?'
>
> The King will reply, 'I tell you the truth, whatever you did for one of the least of these brothers of mine, you did for me' (Mt. 25:34b-40 NIV).

Parker has stepped well outside the comfort zone of the typical 15-year-old and is ministering to the "...least of these brothers..." of Christ. He serves as an example for all of us regarding how Christ expects us to respond to those who are less fortunate or unable to care for themselves. Sometimes that need is emotional instead of physical. Professional caregivers are specially trained to provide comfort to the elderly. Parker is filling a greater need – the need to be loved and to love.

Another example of caring is exemplified by Ranya Kelly, founder and president of Redistribution Center, Inc. Ranya has received many accolades for her mission to feed and clothe the poor, but she doesn't serve for the accolades - she serves because there is a need that isn't being fulfilled through other means. People are hurting and there are too few organizations to assist them through difficult times.

Ranya didn't ***deliberately*** embark on her mission of caring for others. She came upon her opportunity quite by accident in 1991 while looking for a box to mail Christmas presents in. During the search she found 500 pairs of shoes that had been discarded by a local shoe store. Other than being out of season, the shoes were unused. A search for a useful outlet for the shoes brought her to a shelter in suburban Denver. What she found tugged at her heart and changed her life. Halmandaris quotes her, "There was a woman standing in the doorway, her pants dragging on the floor. She was pregnant and barefoot in the middle of January. I couldn't believe it. The look in her eye and her gratitude changed my life" (p. 27).

Ranya's life was changed in a big way. Operating on a budget of $30,000 a year that is entirely funded through donations, she works with local businesses to receive usable, but unsellable, merchandise, food, clothing, building supplies, and other items that the Redistribution Center volunteers redistribute to a variety of organizations, including the Samaritan House, Go-el, Brandon Center, Organization Blessing, and City Harvest, as well as needy individuals, such as soldiers and their families, to name a few. So far the Center has redistributed over $21,000,000 worth of goods. She is quoted on the Redistribution Center Website, "We aren't just providing help to one particular type of individual or organization. We are a link in a chain of giving and contribution that is much bigger than our one organization—we are helping others help the world."

Robert Chapman provided a resting place for missionaries and preachers enroute to doing God's work, and walked the entire country of Spain preaching the Word to the unsaved. Mother Teresa reached out around the world to clothe, feed, and provide medical treatment for the poor. JoAnn, Joannie, and Daniel Cayce have committed their lives to making the lives of widows, orphans, and others in financial distress more bearable in a country that seems too busy for them. Ranya Kelly couldn't just drop off the shoes she found and walk away from the shelter to return to the shelter of her comfort zone. She had to do more. George Washington Carver could have been among the rich and famous, but he chose to accumulate his wealth in a different place and focus his gifts and talents on caring for land and the people whose lives depended on it.

The central theme of each of the people I chose to profile in this chapter is their lack of material wealth and their passion for serving God by reaching out to others in need, whether the need is physical or emotional. Think of how much better our world would be if we all followed their example. I believe it is fitting to close this chapter with more words of love from Mother Teresa.

> At the end of our lives, we will not be judged by how many diplomas we have received, how much money we have made or how many great things we have done. We will be judged by "I was hungry and you gave me to eat. I was naked and you clothed me. I was homeless and you took me in." Hungry not only for bread, but hungry for love. Naked not only for clothing, but naked of human dignity and respect. Homeless not only for want of a room of bricks, but homeless because of rejection. This is Christ in distressing disguise.

Time of Reflection

Read Matthew 25:31-46

- How will you answer the King regarding caring for the needy, widows, and orphans?
- What do you think the feeling of grief will be of those who will not be among the righteous who take their inheritance?
- Reflect on people around you who exemplify caring and sharing as God commanded.
- Why do you think God places so much emphasis on caring for widows and orphans?
- Who do you think God is going to hold accountable for caring for the needy, the sick, the poor, orphans, and widows – government leaders or us as individuals? Qualify and discuss your responses.

Selflessness

> "Do nothing out of selfish ambition or vain conceit, but in humility consider others better than yourselves. Each of you should look not only to your own interests, but also to the interests of others. Your attitude should be the same as that of Christ Jesus."
> - Philippians 2:3-5 (NIV)

One of the themes that I hope will become apparent as this book unfolds is that exhibiting a single Christ-like attribute doesn't make a person like Christ. Associating a person with a single attribute emphasized in one of the chapters is not intended to imply that was the only attribute s/he possessed. Each person from chapter one could be profiled in this chapter as well as any of the future chapters. For instance, JoAnn Cayce is selfless in her mission to others, and she also sacrifices things she could have done or had for herself or her family. Mother Teresa could easily have ignored the plight of the poor and remained inside the relatively comfortable surroundings of the convent school. Instead, she heeded the calling from the Holy Spirit and sacrificed comfort for a life-long mission that brought her more satisfaction than she could otherwise have achieved. However, as I have mentioned before, this book is not about the people profiled, it is about the Christ-like value that is reflected in their story.

I don't know how it is for you, but possibly the most difficult thing for me to do is to put others ahead of myself. Even the disciples had a difficult time with that. Mark tells us that when they had come to Capernaum and were seated in the house, Jesus asked the Twelve,

> 'What were you arguing about on the road?' But they kept quiet because on the way they had argued about who was the greatest. Sitting down, Jesus called the Twelve and said, 'If anyone wants to be first, he must be the very last, and the servant of all' (Mk 9:33-35 NIV).

If we love the Lord, it should be a simple task for us to love one another, but how many of us are truly selfless in our care and concern for others? In his first letter to the Corinthians Paul emphasizes the importance of love. He said,

> If I speak in the tongues of men and of angels, but have not love, I am only a resounding gong of a clanging cymbal. If I have the gift of prophecy and can fathom all mysteries and all knowledge, and if I have a faith that can move mountains, but have not love, I am nothing. If I give all I possess to the poor and surrender my body to the flames, but have not love, I gain nothing. Love is patient, love is kind. It does not envy, it does not boast, it is not proud. It is not rude, it is not self-seeking, it is not easily angered, it keeps no record of wrongs. Love does not delight in evil, but rejoices with the truth. It always protects, always trusts, always hopes, always perseveres. (1Co 13:1-7 NIV)

There was a man, very much like JoAnn Cayce, in Columbia, South Carolina who knew how to love as Paul charged the Corinthians to do. He exemplified selflessness in a way that many of us would like to emulate, but find it difficult to leave our comfort zone for. The man, John Fling (1921 – 2007), didn't want to be in the spotlight, but couldn't stay out of its beam. My awareness of John came about as a result of a 1984 interview profiled by Charles Kuralt on the Simon and Schuster audio titled, Charles Kuralt's Christmas © 1996 Charles Kuralt & CBS Enterprises. John was also mentioned in *Be The Light: A Blueprint For A Happy And Successful Life.*

In Kuralt's interview, John eloquently summed up a charge Jesus passed on to us in Matthew 10:38 and 16:24 by simply stating, "Jesus told us to pick up our cross and follow Him. He didn't say what description it would be, He didn't say how heavy it would be, and He didn't say how far we would have to carry it." Charles Kuralt interviewed a number of people in Columbia who knew John Fling personally. There were stories of him giving away his socks to a man who had none and giving away his coat to a one-legged man who had to walk through the elements to get to the mission every day for a meal. It was said that he gave away three cars, his television set, a watch, and would give away his own money to help people who needed it more than he did. Friends talked about how he would deliver food, run errands, take people to appointments, mow yards, and take kids fishing. John wasn't doing these things for just a few families; he was doing it for dozens of families. At the time of the interview in 1984 he was reported to have been at his mission for twenty years with no time off. In John's words, "...I don't think we need to wait until we die to enjoy a little of God's kingdom right here on earth."

Bill Halmandaris went further in his presentation of the values John held so near and dear. Bill found that Fling, one of 19 children, grew up on the banks of the Chattahoochee River. John told him, "Our family was so poor we weren't even sharecroppers. We were sharecropper's helpers. What we ate, we had to scavenge, catch out of the water, dig out of the ground, or shake out of a tree" (p. 217). Bill cited that even though John had only a third grade education he understood more than most of us about the world around us and that he possessed a genuine desire to make a difference.

Too often we think, "if I only had money I could do so much good for others." John never had any money of his own, except for a small savings to cover funeral expenses for him and his wife. In fact, he didn't even have a home of his own, although he helped other people buy homes for themselves. His desire to give to others was exceeded only by his passion to do God's work. John was quoted as saying, "My mission in life is making the lives of others easier" (Swanson, 1997).

Bill called John the "Saint of South Carolina." He said, "All he does is whatever needs doing for an extended family that includes four hundred children, two hundred seniors, and about forty blind people. Every day John Fling goes looking for someone else to help. He buys food, delivers food and laundry, transports the needy to medical appointments, and responds to dozens of calls from people in need . . ." (p. 216).

John operated his ministry from his cottage home, located behind the home of his mother-in-law, but it reached out to people all across

Columbia. To John Fling, helping others in a loving, kind, generous, patient way is the responsibility of every man. It's a shame that feeling is getting so watered down with passing generations – or is it?

I didn't get to know John Fling personally and that saddens me. But there is someone close to me who humbles me in the same way. Through my daughter, Lori, I am learning that there are many John Flings around us who quietly go about sharing God's love in so many wonderful ways without pride or boasting.

Lori is a single-parent who has worked hard to provide for herself and her son. It hasn't been easy, but the fruits of her labor have been blessed by a bountiful harvest of God's love around the world. Lori has developed a trust in, and reliance on, the Lord that cements her belief that all things *are* possible through Him.

In the late 1990s, Lori felt a calling to get involved in short-term mission work in Mexico. It wasn't enough for her to send money or clothing. She had to become immersed in the work in the most desperate area possible – the dumps around Mexico City. Lori is not the adventurous type so when she told me about the work she was going to do I knew the Holy Spirit had to be at work in her. In fact, she told me later that her involvement was truly at the prompting of the voice of the Lord. She is sure He actually spoke to her while she was sitting in the church pew. When she embarked on her first mission trip she had no idea what was in store, but she was sure God was moving her in that direction and that He would reveal everything she needed to know when she needed to know it. The Mexico missions allowed her to serve others while serving the Lord. But the mission work doesn't end there.

When she returned from her first trip to Mexico, she felt another calling. This time it was to get involved in mission work closer to home. In her words, "I got involved in working at the rescue mission because the reality that other single mothers were raising their children there reminded me it could have been me. I admire the men and women so much who seek shelter and meals there because asking for help is the hardest thing to do. It is our human nature to view ourselves as failures because we had to ask for help. I just wanted to take the opportunity to let the mission residents know they are special. I have found that to lend a helping hand doesn't require us to travel across the ocean. Again, I believe God was moving me in this direction."

About that same time, Lori decided to open her home to exchange students. Over the years she has hosted students from Germany, France, Russia, and Turkey. If they didn't have a heart for Jesus when they arrived, they sure did when they left. She has involved them all in her local mission work. Lori is changing the world one life at a time.

Following her exposure to a student from the Muslim religion she decided she had to journey to Turkey to evangelize for the Lord. Her mission trip lasted about a month and included street-corner evangelism in Ireland and then on to Turkey where she stayed with the family of her exchange student. Although she hasn't converted that family yet, they are open for her to return to share God's Word with them again.

Every mission trip has been funded by her personally through donations and contributions. No matter how much the cost financially, she has trusted in the Lord to provide. He has showered His blessings upon her and provided a number of miracles along the way.

Recently Lori completed the biggest mission of her life. Through a Vacation Bible School sponsorship program in the spring of 2008, she hosted a Russian orphan. The thirteen year old girl was considered unadoptable because of her age. At first Lori rationalized that she couldn't possibly afford to adopt Inna, but a few months after Inna returned to her orphanage the Holy Spirit moved Lori to begin the adoption journey.

Lori confided that part of the motivation was the result of her work at the shelter. She said, "Actually, it was seeing the teen boys at the men's shelter who had just come out of the foster care system with no where else to go that made me begin to think about adoption, or made me listen to God prompting me to adopt."

After almost fifteen months of planning, and $45,000 worth of fundraising and witnessing the awesome presence of the Lord in our lives, Inna was welcomed to our family. What a blessing it is to have her in our lives. There is now one more life dedicated to Christ.

Lori and John have spent their lives in selfless service, but selflessness comes in many forms, shapes, and sizes. A person's Cross may impact many lives, or a single life. I don't think **anyone's** Cross impacts only one life though. Our selfless act might be focused on a single life, but the radiance of selflessness can illuminate the lives of people around us that we don't even know we are reaching. Here are a few people whose individual acts of selflessness have impacted my life and lives of people around me. I'm sure you can think of similar examples.

George Washington Carver once said, "When you do the common things in life in an uncommon way, you will command the attention of the world" (BrainyQuote, 2010). Well, Milton (Mick) Doane hasn't commanded the attention of the world, at least not the world outside our small community, but he does common things in an uncommon way. Mick and his wife, Betty, are members of our church. Mick is 86 years old at this writing and he has lived on the same property all of his life. In our small community it's hard to hide or to hide anything that you don't want the neighbors to know about, not that Mick or Betty ever had anything to hide. Their lives have been dedicated to the Lord for more years than anyone can remember. They didn't consider themselves as missionaries, but their work within our community resembled a mission to us. Mick retired from a career as a TV repairman and was handy at just about anything. If anyone had a problem with a mower, appliance, plumbing, or anything else around the house, they could always rely on Mick to not only be able to fix it, but he would likely have the part in his garage. He had more uncommon stuff in his garage than a hardware store. That wasn't all that was uncommon about Mick and Betty though. Neither of them made an impact on the national scene, but the uncommon, selfless love they demonstrated for each other and the people around them made them heroes to all of us.

Betty developed dementia in the late 1990s and as she slowly progressed to Alzheimer's, Mick was continually by her side. He fed her, dressed her, cooked and cleaned, cared for her every need, helped her sit down, helped her stand up, helped her walk, and helped lift her legs to get into and out of the car when she could no longer control her own movements. His love for her was a constant inspiration to everyone who knew their situation, and his devotion to her was a reminder to the men of our church just what the marriage covenant is intended to mean. Like John Fling, Mick was carrying a Cross heavier and farther than any of us men who admire him so much hope to have to carry it ourselves. We all feel so inadequate to the task. Mick didn't mind caring for Betty. It kept them together, which made the burden a blessing. It was not until Betty was in need of Hospice that Mick turned the responsibility of her care over to anyone else. But he was never far from her side. They were married over 60 years and were in love every day.

In other chapters I will profile a few of the invisible military heroes who have devoted, and sometimes dedicated, their lives in a selfless mission to keep our country safe. One of them, Dave Irwin, is not well known, and he prefers it that way. He is just someone like your neighbor, teacher, friend, or relative. What sets him apart in a selfless way is how he puts the needs of others ahead of his own.

Dave was raised in a family where selflessness was the norm. One day on a rice-paddy battle field, then Lt. Irwin, almost lost his life exemplifying that attribute. Lt. Irwin would make a decision over the course of that day that would have a profound impact on the rest of his life. His platoon was pinned down in an intense fire-fight. As he directed evacuations of the wounded, called in artillery and air support, and managed his forces against the enemy, he was severely wounded himself. He lost much of the inside of his thigh when he exposed himself to retrieve ammunition. Bleeding profusely, he continued to direct the operations of his platoon and refused evacuation until everyone in his platoon could be extracted from the area. He doesn't talk about that experience much. I served with him for twenty years following Vietnam so I had many opportunities to see the wound first-hand. I also had the opportunity to see his life transformed as he followed in Christ's footsteps. As a Christian counselor, Dave continues to put the needs of others ahead of his own. Like Lori, God is using him to transform lives one at a time.

Do you remember the "good old days" when shopping was done in a neighborhood grocery store and after selecting your items you told the cashier to "charge it" to your account? We had such a store in our neighborhood for more than sixty years. It was owned and operated by a wonderful gentleman named Albert M. Mansor (1898 – 1981). Al, as we affectionately called him, was from Aramta, a small village in Lebanon. He immigrated to the United States in 1913 at the age of 15 following his mother's death. His uncle owned a grocery store near our neighborhood and Al started work for him upon his arrival. Al worked in the store during the day and attended night school to learn English and study for citizenship.

Al's uncle died shortly after World War I and Al was left with a debt of $4,000. Soon after that a tornado hit the neighborhood and destroyed the store. He was beside himself with grief and was advised to seek legal advice. His lawyer said his only alternative was bankruptcy. Al became enraged over the lawyer's recommendation for an easy way out and told him he would repay everything he owed. His faith in God forbade him to break a bond of honor. Since he lived in an apartment behind the store, he now had no place to live as well. God came to his rescue in the form of an elderly neighbor lady who took him in until he could get back on his feet.

He lost the property that the store was on, but again God was faithful. An ice company gave him a small horse shed that he moved onto a vacant piece of land where neighbors helped him turn the shed into a grocery store. Handshake loans from wholesale grocery companies and his friends helped him through four years of rebuilding, but at the end of that time he was able to repay all of his debt. He spent the rest of his life helping others, to repay the kindness shown him.

Although Al didn't have any children of his own, he loved the children in our neighborhood. His store was across the street from the grade school so he knew all of the children by name and reputation. To encourage good work in school, Al would pay the kids for good grades and would host trips to the movie for kids that had good report cards, until the groups got so large he couldn't transport them all. Then he decided to hold a summer picnic in the local park where all of the children received a meal, played games, and got free pony rides.

Every Thanksgiving Al would make up baskets of food for those who he knew were in need. He gave an apple tree to every child so that they could have something to care for and call their very own. A friend described Al as, "a bachelor with an abundance of worldly goods and could have had a bigger store and more money, but this wasn't his measure of success in this world because his life was dedicated to his fellow man, especially the community he lived in, and this love and friendship was returned a thousand fold by all. This man's life was giving, not getting."

During the Great Depression Al sold groceries on a hand shake. That trust of his fellow man was the essence of his philosophy for a good life. That was to love people, be truthful in all things, not to worry, and always think positively. Al's final act of love for his neighbors was the donation of the land his store was on to the school so the children could have a larger playground. Al was selfless to a fault. (J. Assid, personal communication, September 19, 2002).

John Fling demonstrated God's love through his mission of running errands, providing comfort, and helping people buy homes and cars so they could be independent. Lori brought kindness, clothing, hope, and encouragement to people in the dumps of Mexico City. Mick cared for his wife in a way that all of us admired, but few could duplicate. Dave gave up his opportunity for evacuation from the battlefield numerous times so other soldiers could be airlifted to field hospitals first. Al put others first, encouraged youngsters to excel, and dedicated his life to selfless acts of kindness. In each case, selflessness was a physical act of help or kindness for people known and unknown to the person bringing aid. There is another form of selflessness that is equally as healing for both the giver and the receiver. I call it inspirational selflessness – focusing on the emotional needs of others, even when you are in need yourself.

Have you ever noticed how a terminally ill person who has Christ at the center of their life always seems to be more concerned about the needs of those around them than they are for their own situation? I think I know where that inner peace comes from, but I am always in awe when I witness it. My first experience with a terminally ill person greatly influenced my own transformation to a life with Christ. Her name was Sarah Six. Sarah was an administrative assistant at the company where my wife, Pat, and I worked. Sarah had been diagnosed with breast cancer about five years before we met her. She had a mastectomy followed by chemotherapy and was in remission for some time. Not long after we met her the cancer returned. She underwent treatment again and continued to work. I recall that she never would dwell on her own issues, but she was constantly praying for the needs and care of those around her. She might not have been full of life, but she was full of Christ's love. Our company routinely recognized outstanding employees quarterly and annually. Shortly after Sarah's death she was recognized as the employee of the quarter and later as the employee of the year. There was no doubt that Sarah's compassion, caring, concern, and love impacted hundreds of people around her that she never had a chance to know, but they all knew about Sarah Six.

By following God's commands to trust and obey Him, all of these people have wound up richer than anyone on the widely acclaimed lists of wealthiest people in the world. Their wealth has been stored in heaven along with that of all of the other selfless, caring, sharing heroes who quietly go about putting the needs of others ahead of their own.

Time of Reflection

Read Jeremiah 7:23; Matthew 6:25-34; and Romans 14:7-8 and discuss the following questions:

- What are some additional examples of selflessness in Jesus life? How about in Paul's life?
- Describe how selflessness is demonstrated in the life of a person you hold in highest regard.
- Is selflessness an attribute that others can see in your life? What are some examples?
- What are some of the things you worry about? Do you believe you can lay them at the foot of the Cross and walk away with the assurance that He will take care of them?

Discipleship

> Therefore go and make disciples of all nations, baptizing
> them in the name of the Father and of the Son and of the Holy Spirit,
> and teaching them to obey everything I have commanded you.
> and surely I am with you always, to the very end of the age.
> - Matthew 28:19-20 (NIV)

Jesus was speaking to the disciples when He gave them what has come to be known as the "Great Commission." Was He speaking only to them or is that message for all of us? Do you need to be ordained to bring someone to Christ? Can only the ordained baptize? Those are questions that many denominations interpret differently. John the Baptist was not ordained by man, he was ordained by God. Ordination through a seminary is our modern definition of how a priest, pastor, preacher should be schooled to minister to the flock, but the Bible doesn't require that. Elders and Deacons are selected by a body of Christians or they are called by the Holy Spirit to serve. I believe God intended the Great Commission for every person who has accepted Jesus as his or her Lord and Savior.

The pastor of the church I attend regularly when I am working in Kentucky has been a blessing to me as I write this book. The Holy Spirit is alive in that church. As I was working on this chapter the title of his sermon was, "Can I Make a Difference." It fit perfectly with discipleship. He covered three main topics that were already part of this chapter, but I didn't realize it. I am continually at awe with how the Holy Spirit works within us. The three points for making a difference in another person's understanding of the Word and bringing that person to a personal relationship with Christ are:

1. **I must be competent** – I must have a personal relationship with Christ, and I must be able to use the Word in response to the persons concerns, apprehensions, and doubts.
2. **I must be confident** – I must be able to speak authoritatively. I must have the assurance that my walk with Christ is a living example of the Word.

3. **I must be courageous** – I must be able to step out in faith and speak boldly of the Love of Christ for others. Our courage comes from the confidence of knowing that God is with us just as we was with the chosen people of Israel when he told them through the prophet Isaiah, 'Fear not, for I have redeemed you: I have called you by name, you are mine. When you pass through the waters, I will be with you, and through the rivers, they shall not overwhelm you; when you walk through fire you shall not be burned, and the flame shall not consume you. For I am the Lord your God, the Holy One of Israel, your Savior" (Isaiah 43:1b-3a ESV). (S. Wilson, Pastor, personal communication, December, 2009).

It's no coincidence that the words disciple and discipline are so similar in spelling and so connected in a life for Christ. As I researched the story behind Teen Challenge, which is detailed later in the chapter, it struck me that a lack of discipline is the environment that Satan calls home for *his* disciples, while the presence of discipline is fundamental for disciples for Christ. A lack of discipline breeds arrogance, which can lead a person to believe that the world is about them and that they are autonomous – capable of doing everything on their own and not dependent on anyone. On the other hand, the presence of discipline in our lives causes us to be aware of how dependent we are on God and how all that we are and all that we have is a reflection of His blessings upon us. In Deuteronomy 8:3 Moses reminded the Israelites that, "He humbled you, causing you to hunger and then feeding you with manna, which neither you nor your fathers had known, to teach you that man does not live by bread alone but on every word that comes from the mouth of the Lord" (NIV).

So if we are commanded to be disciples for Christ, and we are confident, competent, and courageous we should be responding to God's call. What keeps many of us from responding? You can ponder that again later during the time of reflection, but it might have something to do with our general reluctance to move outside of our comfort zone. The following are examples of people who have stepped out in faith and exemplify the Great Commission.

John 13:34-35 (ESV) states, "A new commandment I give to you, that you love one another: just as I have loved you, you also are to love one another. By this all people will know that you are my disciples, if you have love for one another." There is something special about the innocent love that children have the ability to display that loses its luster in "mature" adults. One example of that love, Daniel Cayce, was shared in an earlier chapter. There is another disciple that I want to introduce you to now. His name is Zach Bonner. Zach is 12 years old and has been sharing love with others for six years. Wikipedia describes Zach as, "an American philanthropist" (*Zach Bonner:* Wikipedia, 2010). I have always considered philanthropy to be something that the rich engage in, but Merriam-Webster.com defines philanthropy additionally as an "active effort to promote human welfare" (philanthropy, 2010). In that context, Zach is the essence of philanthropy.

Zach's mission started in the aftermath of Hurricane Charley in 2004. When he heard about the shortage of water that some of the people in his area were experiencing, he took his little red wagon and started walking the neighborhoods asking people to share some of their stockpile with those who were in need. Within a short time he had collected 27 pick-up truck loads of water for redistribution.

The following year Zach tackled a bigger challenge. He founded Little Red Wagon Foundation, a non-profit charity organization. His mission now is to provide aid to the 1.3 million homeless children in the United States. Wikipedia quotes Zach, "These kids don't have a home, they don't have a safe place to sleep at night. They're out on the streets not because they want to be, but because it's out of their control." Zach is trying to help them get control of their lives again. In 2007 he organized an awareness campaign known simply as 24 Hours. He enlists high school students who are willing to spend 24 hours in a box simulating life on the streets for the homeless. He isn't satisfied with just making people aware of their plight; his goal is to provide permanent shelter for all the homeless children. Zach wants to build homes for them or find apartments for them and their families. To raise the money to reach his goal he has already completed a project he called "My House to the White House." My House to the White House was a walking trip that Zach completed in three segments during the summers. In 2006 Zach walked from his home in Tampa, FL to Tallahassee. Then in 2007 he walked from Tallahassee to Atlanta. He completed the final leg from Atlanta to Washington, DC in 2008. The objective of the trip was to raise funds to his mission. That was a good start for his campaign, but now he is setting the bar higher. In April 2010 he will begin the nearly 2,500 mile trek from Tampa, FL. to Los Angeles, CA. Along the way he plans to work on projects to aid homeless children. He calls this one "Coast to Coast Walk – One Boy's Journey to End Youth Homelessness" (*Zach Bonner:* Wikipedia, 2010).

Zach recently received Beliefnet's "Most Inspiring Person of 2009" award for compassionate, selfless service to homeless children. In an interview following the award ceremony he was asked about some of the ways his organization has been of service to homeless children. Zack said,

> Well, there was this one boy, his name was Chris. It was when we first started with the backpack program. With the backpacks, we put a food pack, a personal hygiene kit, a sewing kit, a first-aid kit, a candy pack, and a small toy. This boy received a backpack. He (was) pulling out the food and the personal hygiene and the sewing kit and all that stuff, the basic necessities. But then he pulled out the candy pack and the toy. And the organization that we were working with at that time said that was the first time that they had seen him smile in the whole entire time that they had been working with him. He said that that was the first toy that he had gotten in as long as he could remember. And that's just one of the stories that we've heard from the different organizations that we've been working with, that the backpacks or different projects that we do, the holiday parties or stuff like that, have impacted families and children. (Brockway, 2010).

The Bible tells us about another twelve-year-old who shook the world to action when he challenged the status quo. That was the young Christ Jesus who went into the temple to listen to the teachers and question them. Zach isn't questioning us yet, but he is challenging us.

Upon hearing of Zach's final stage of his walk to the White House, one woman wrote,

> I love to give as you do! I was taught as a young girl to always share, now it is my life's work. I know that people get the resources when you track it properly. I praise God for these types of children. I teach and I know from experience that children have a love and desire to help and give. I pray that you will reach your goals and shatter all expectations. I am sending my contribution to your efforts. May God bless and protect you as you walk from your house to the White House. It is amazing what one person can do to make a difference (ypwr.blogs.cnn.com, 2009).

That sums up Zach's discipleship pretty well. I'm confident that the people Zack ministers to will one day reach out and share God's love with others just as Zack has done for them.

Probably the most notable modern-day traditional interpretation of a disciple for Christ is Billy Graham. In his book *Just as I Am,* Billy Graham describes how he wasn't always a Christian. There was a time when he was going through the motions like most of us do before God finally gets a firm hold on our life. He recounts that on one occasion in 1934, when he was sixteen, his father allowed a local group to use his pasture for an all-day prayer meeting of scripture, singing, and evangelism. When Billy and a friend heard the singing, Billy commented, "I guess they're some fanatics that have talked Daddy into using the place" (p. 27). Some time later, his father told him that prayers went up that day for a person to be raised up from the Charlotte area to preach the gospel to all corners of the world. Little did Billy know what the Holy Spirit had in store for him.

In the summer of that year, Dr. Mordecai Ham held a series of revivals in Charlotte. Initially Billy didn't want to attend, but his mother prodded him and a friend, Grady Wilson, to go. Billy attended several of the revivals and professed his faith before the end of the summer. His dedication to his new faith remained cool for some time though. Billy became a Fuller Brush salesman before attending Bible college. He wasn't very comfortable in the college environment and had difficulty applying himself to his studies. He dropped out of one college after a short time, but was encouraged to continue because God had a purpose for him. Billy discovered that he had a way of connecting with people through his speaking ability which renewed his interest in studies.

He started preaching before finishing college and at one of his revivals at the First Baptist Church of East Palatka, FL. it became known that Billy hadn't been baptized himself. He announced that he would be baptized with all of the new believers at the end of the revival series. Even though young Billy Graham hadn't been ordained, or even baptized himself, God was using him to make disciples of all nations, and over the years, Billy has done just that. There is hardly a nation on Earth that hasn't hosted a Billy Graham crusade. Although there have been some controversies in his life, there is no doubt that the prayer that was lifted up that day at the service in his father's field has been answered. It was reported that as of 2008 his lifetime audience topped 2.2 billion people (*Billy Graham:* Wikipedia, 2010). That's an amazing outreach for Christ Jesus considering the man who accomplished it was initially reluctant to give his life to the Lord.

Bishop Fulton J. Sheen (1895 – 1979) was a TV evangelist before the term became popular. He hosted a night-time radio program, *The Catholic Hour,* for 20 years before moving to television in 1951 to host *Life is Worth Living* (1951 – 1957). The format of the original television program was revived as *The Fulton Sheen Program* from 1961 to 1968. Although I wasn't Catholic, I found Bishop Sheen captivating, with a charisma that had me hanging on to every word, and I wasn't alone. The radio program reached an estimated 4 million listeners and the television programs had a weekly audience of 30 million (Archbishop Fulton J. Sheen, 2010).

Bishop Sheen had a way of delivering a message that made the Bible interesting, and since the King James version was about the only translation available when I was beginning to watch the program, that was necessary to disciple a teen who didn't understand the lofty language of the King James Bible. His programs were not about promoting Catholicism; they were about spreading the Word as Jesus had directed the disciples to do. The denominational neutrality of his message was probably what made him so popular. In fact, he was so popular that he won an Emmy Award for *Most Outstanding Television Personality* in 1952, defeating Edward R. Murrow, Lucille Ball, and Arthur Godfrey for the award. That was quite an accomplishment considering his program was opposite Milton Berle, who basically owned Tuesday night television. But I suppose it wasn't fair competition considering Bishop Sheen had Jesus as his director/producer. When he accepted the award he thanked his four writers for their inspiring words – Matthew, Mark, Luke, and John. Many famous people like Bishop Sheen have volumes of quotes attributed to them, but he chose to preach the volumes of quotes by our Lord and Savior, Jesus Christ. It is pretty hard to top His quotes.

Discipleship can take an indirect approach like Zach's, a direct approach like Billy Graham and Bishop Fulton J. Sheen, or a combination of the two. Bill Gaither and Pat Boone come to mind as representing the latter scenario. Although Bill and Pat are from the same generation, and their careers have arrived at about the same point, their paths have been much different.

Bill Gaither started his career with discipleship through music as his mission. Although he pursued a teaching profession for a while, that only got in the way of his real passion of bringing the Gospel to people through music. He was among the pioneers of modern contemporary Christian music. In the Holiday classic, *It's a Wonderful Life,* Clarence reminds George that each person's life touches so many others. Bill Gaither's life is a wonderful example of that. He has been a father figure to many current contemporary artists such as Mark Lowry, Michael W. Smith, Sandi Patti, Carman, Steve Green, Don Francisco, Amy Grant, Michael English, Jonathan Pierce, Karla Worley, and Cynthia Clawson. Together they bring Christ to millions of people around the world who might not otherwise experience His grace and love (*Bill Gaither,* Wikipedia 2010).

Like everyone else being profiled in this book, Pat Boone could fit anywhere, but because his journey with the Lord took a number of turns, I chose to include him in the chapter on repentance.

One of the most inspiring people I found in my research is a young man named Nick Vujicic. Nick is a preacher-evangelist, stock investor, real estate investor, author, motivational speaker, and mission director. What is most inspiring about Nick is what he considers as his gift from God. You see, Nick was born without arms or legs, but he has more energy, drive, passion, and love for God than most people you will meet in a life time.

Lawn Griffiths, reporter for the *East Valley Tribune,* a Mesa, AZ. newspaper wrote this about a speech Nick made at Gateway Fellowship Church in Gilbert, AZ., in February 2007,

> "I stand before you today as a miracle of God," said Nick Vujicic. "By the end of this service, you are going to be jealous of my life," he said wryly. Blending stories of freely traveling the world without limbs, he made himself an example that being human is a rich experience, even if he is mostly limited to a head and torso. Vujicic has spoken live to about 1.7 million people in 12 countries in the past 2 1/2 years and tens of millions via TV.
>
> "I can smile. You can't undo my joy, you can't undo my faith," he said. "I feel the joy, strength and victory in my life," he proclaimed, as he repeatedly told his audience that "God is your friend," worthy of being praised through the hardest times. Again and again, he told people to look past daily setbacks and complaints and recognize God's constant love for them.
>
> "When people see me for the first time, they sort of freak out, especially the children," he said. "A little boy comes up to me one day and goes, 'What happened?' so I said, 'Cigarettes.' Another time a 2 1/2-year-old girl was asked to give Vujicic a hug. She thought it through, then put her hands

tightly behind her back 'and she hugged me with her neck,' he said." That kind of selfless inspiration is hard to deny. Nick says that God has transformed him, "from life without limbs to life without limits."

What a wonderful world this would be if we all adopted that mantra.
Lawn quoted Nick asking the audience,

> "Let me ask you: If God answered every one of your prayers right now, on a scale of 1 to 10, with 10 being the highest, where would your joy be? ... Is God not good now? Is God not worthy of your praise, now?" It seems to me that the most joyful people are those that spend their life unselfishly aspiring to meet the needs of others. God commanded the Israelites to, 'Give generously to him [your needy brother] and do so without a grudging heart; then because of this the Lord your God will bless you in all your work and in everything you put your hand to.' Dt. 15:10-11 (NIV). In verse 14b, He commanded, 'Give to him as the Lord your God has blessed you.'"

Nick seems to be giving more than God blessed **him** with. Maybe he is making up for those who haven't yet recognized the gifts God has blessed them with.
Lawn closes her article as Nick closed the program that night,

> "Aren't you jealous of my life yet?" he asked the audience. "You are seeing that I am living a purpose. God has a purpose for you." Shouting and leaning intently forward, Vujicic said, "God has a purpose for you to love. To love people. There are people in hospitals who want visits. There are hungry people waiting to be fed. Find a means that [sic] to love them. Do you know how

to do that? That is what the church is for" (Griffiths, 2007).

I haven't attended one of Nick's programs, but I am now asking myself, What purpose am I serving? How am I using His blessings to fulfill God's will? Am I demonstrating real love towards others? Am I making disciples of all nations? It's time to stop asking and start acting.

In his book *The Cross and the Switchblade* (Wilkerson, 1962) David Wilkerson states, "As far as I know, since the days when clergymen first started to marry in the Christian Church, there has always been a Wilkerson in the ministry, and usually in a fiery ministry, too" (p.35). That's a lot of opportunity for discipleship. The big difference between David's discipleship and that of other evangelists is who David evangelizes to. David Wilkerson is the founder of Teen Challenge, but he acknowledges that it is the Holy Spirit that enables the ministry to reach an audience around the world. David learned early to get out of the way and allow God's will to unfold through the Holy Spirit.

David's story is the most remarkable I've ever read. I came across David Wilkerson while I was researching Pat Boone. Pat picked up David's book in an airport terminal and was as awestruck by the story as I was. Pat immediately wanted to make the book into a movie, but had to be patient while the Holy Spirit worked in the people who would eventually partner with Pat in the production. That's another story that I don't intend to detail here.

David's story is so filled with miracles and the working of the Holy Spirit that only a Bible-believing Christian can read it and say, "Yes! Yes!" Others may read the book or see the movie and pass it off as Hollywood sensationalism, when in fact the story represents the Holy Spirit working in and through real people.

Although David doesn't mention it in his book, my perception is that his ministry is rooted in the Psalms, specifically Psalm 1 and 119. Psalm 1:1-2 states, "Blessed is the man who does not walk in the counsel of the wicked or stand in the way of sinners or sit in the seat of mockers. But his delight is in the law of the Lord, and on his law he meditates day and night" (NIV). Psalm 119 is pretty much the whole Bible wrapped up in one chapter. It happens to be the longest chapter in the Bible and is mid way through the Old and New Testaments. Regarding Psalm 119 my NIV Study Bible notes, "A devotional on the word of God. The author was an Israelite of exemplary piety (probably postexilic) who (1) was passionately devoted to the word of God as the word of life; (2) humbly acknowledged, nevertheless, the errant ways of his heart and life; (3) knew the pain – but also the fruits – of God's corrective discipline; and (4) had suffered much at the hands of those who arrogantly disregarded God's word and made him the target of their hostility, ridicule and slander" (p. 906). David's calling would require him to draw upon the discipline of the Psalmist in order for him to discipline others and for them to be disciples as well.

In February, 1958, Davie, as the people he ministered to called him, was pastor of a country church in Pennsylvania. A story in Life magazine caught his attention and changed his life forever. The story was about a cruel murder of a young handicapped man by a gang of teens in New York City. Davie felt compassion for the victim and his family, but his heart also went out to the teens that had committed such a heinous crime. After all, all of the people involved were God's children, and He loved them all equally. Davie says he was compelled by the Holy Spirit to not only reach out to those boys, but to all of the lost souls and lonely young people involved in drugs, narcotics, murder, robbery, prostitution, and other crimes in NYC.

The events surrounding David's journey to NYC and subsequent work there are detailed in his book in a very moving way. I couldn't help but feel the Holy Spirit within the pages of that book. His story is inspiring, but the results are incredible. How incredible can only be conveyed by quoting a testimonial from one of the gang members David reached through his ministry. This particular gang member had threatened to kill David, but that didn't deter David from sharing God's love with him in a convincing way. David details the young man's testimony that was first shared at the initial Teen Challenge fund raising event. David recorded the young man's story as:

> I was mostly in the streets," he began, "because my parents had customers coming where we lived. They would come at night or in the day and then

all of us kids had to go out. They were spiritualists, my parents. They advertised in the Spanish papers that they would talk to the dead and cure sickness, and they would also give advice about money and family problems.

There was only one room at home, so us kids were in the streets. At first the other kids beat me up all the time and I was afraid. Then I learned how to fight and they were scared of me and they left me alone. After a while I got so I liked it better in the streets than I did at home. At home I was the youngest one. I was nothing. But in the street they knew who I was.

My family moved a lot and mostly it was on account of me. If there was any trouble the police would come around asking questions and then the superintendent wherever we lived would go to my parents and say we had to move. They didn't want their building to have trouble with the police. It was that way if the police just asked a Puerto Rican boy a question. It didn't matter if he did anything, the minute the police came around asking about him, he and his family had to get out.

I didn't know why I acted like I did. There was a thing inside me that scared me. It worried me all the time but I couldn't stop it. It was this feeling I got if I saw a cripple. It was a feeling like I wanted to kill him. It was that way with blind people too, or real little kids – anyone weak or hurt - I would hate them.

One day I told my old man about this thing. We never talked or anything but this thing scared me. So I told him and he said I had a devil. He tried to call the devil out of me, but it wouldn't come.

The crazy thing in me got worse and worse. If someone had crutches I would kick them or if an old man had a beard I would try to pull it out and I would rough up little kids. And all the while I

> would be scared and wanting to cry, but the thing inside me was laughing and laughing. The other thing was blood. The minute I saw blood I would begin to laugh and I couldn't stop it.
>
> When we moved into the Fort Greene Projects, I went in with the Mau Maus. They wanted me to be President. But in a rumble the President was to direct traffic (give orders) and I wanted to fight. So they made me Vice-President (p.86 – 87).

The young man went on to tell how he would fight so aggressively that even his own gang members stayed out of his way. He learned how to use a knife and had stuck 16 people and been in jail twelve times. Everyone knew about his reputation. He told of an incident when he was attacked by five boys and was strangled so hard that his voice box was damaged. He calmly told about a gang fight in a candy store in which a rival gang member and one of the owners was killed. After the killings his parents became so scared of him that they returned to Puerto Rico and the young man was left with only his gang friends to care for him.

Shortly after that the young man had his first encounter with David. The young man's story continues:

> I turned eighteen in July 1958. That month the Dragons from the Red Hook projects killed one of our boys. We were going down on the subway to get one of them. That's gang law: if one Mau Mau dies, one Dragon dies. We were walking down Edward Street on our way to the subway station when we saw a police car stopped and a whole bunch of Chaplains hanging around.
>
> It looked like action so we headed over. The Chaplains were all standing around two guys I never seen, one had a bugle and the other was a real skinny guy (p. 88).

The skinny guy, David, was beginning his street corner evangelizing in the heart of the gang districts. David's message proved to be a life changing experience for some of the gang leaders that day, but this young man wanted nothing to do with it. However, David was persistent. He kept returning to the streets sharing the Word of God and wearing down the resistance of the tough gang members. This young man's life changed during a rally that his gang attended for the purpose of making trouble, but the Holy Spirit had a different outcome in store for him.

David selected members from the Mau Maus to collect the offering at the rally. The young man was one of those selected and his intention was to make off with the money and make David look like a fool. What he didn't count on was the Holy Spirit causing him to respond in kind to David's trust and confidence in him.

He concluded his testimonial with the emotional experience that followed.

> Well, I went back to my seat and I was thinking harder than I ever thought before. He started talking and it was all about the Holy Spirit. The preacher said the Holy Spirit could get inside people and make them clean. He said it didn't matter what they'd done, the Holy Spirit could make them start new, like babies.
> Suddenly I wanted that so bad I couldn't stand it. It was as if I was seeing myself for the first time. All the filth and the hate and the foulness like pictures in front of my eyes.
> 'You can be different!' he said. 'Your life can be changed.'
> I wanted that, I needed that, but I knew it couldn't happen to me. The preacher told us to come forward if we wanted to be changed but I knew it was no use for me.
> Then Israel told us all to get up. 'I'm President,' he said, 'and this whole gang is going up there!'
> I was the first one at the rail. I kneeled down and said the first prayer of my life and this was it: 'Dear God, I'm the dirtiest sinner in New York. I don't think You want me. If You do want me,

> You can have me. As bad as I was before, I want to be that good for Jesus' (p. 90 - 91).

David's ministry was overwhelmingly successful from the start. However, he recognized that many of the converts didn't have a disciplined home life or a relationship with someone who could mentor them in the early phase of their walk with Christ and therefore they succumbed to Satan's temptations and returned to their old ways. They didn't have the discipline of dependence on God. Recalling the need for discipline in our lives, David developed a regimen for those seeking salvation that included hours of Bible study, chapel time, witnessing to others through testimonials, general educational studies, chores in the Center, and other duties that focused on fellowship within the community of believers. That regimen continues today and is the reason for Teen Challenge's success rate in turning people from lives of crime, drugs, prostitution, etc., to lives dedicated to Christ.

David Wilkerson brought thousands of lost and lonely young people to Christ in the first few years of his ministry in NYC and many of them have gone on to become ministers who are evangelizing to many more thousands of people around the world. The young man that David introduced to the Holy Spirit at that rally was Nicky Cruz. Today Nicky is helping others develop a relationship with Christ through his own ministry in troubled neighborhoods in Europe and the United States.

Each year my home church hosts a Teen Challenge Sunday that is filled with joy and fellowship as students share how the Holy Spirit is transforming their lives. They may not be aware that through their testimonies they transform our lives as well. Discipleship is not a one way street. The person ministering receives as much joy from the Holy Spirit as the one being ministered to.

It's important to again reflect on the quote from *It's a Wonderful Life* that I introduced at the beginning of this chapter. George learned from the angel Clarence that each person's life touches so many others. The discipleship examples, and others in this book, demonstrate how right Clarence was. Shouldn't we all be touching lives with Christ in our hearts? What a wonderful world we would be living in then.

Time of Reflection
Read Matthew 10:37-38; 11:12; Mark 1:17; 9:50; Luke 9:23-27

- Jesus' words in Matthew 10:37-38 seem very harsh and uncaring. What does Jesus expect from us when he refers to taking up our Cross?
- Matthew 11:12 refers to forceful men laying hold to the kingdom of heaven. That could be interpreted two ways. One is that Satan is trying to beat down discipleship and the other is godly people battling Satan for control. Discuss those interpretations and any other you see emerging from that reading.
- Jesus invited Simon and Andrew to become fishers of men. He invites us to do the same. Discuss the implication of that invitation and why so few respond.
- Mark 9:50 talks about salt. Discuss what David Wilkerson discovered about salt losing its saltiness when new Christians returned to their old world. How can the saltiness be restored?
- In Luke, Jesus challenges us again to take up our Cross. He says, "I tell you the truth, some who are standing here will not taste death before they see the kingdom of God." Since the Bible is a book for all time, discuss how that message should be interpreted by Christians today.

Sacrifice/Trust

"Greater love has no one than this,
that he lay down his life for his friends."
-John 15:13 (NIV)

This chapter has been dual titled to emphasize a point that is so critical when we consider the sacrifices people have made, and continue to make, when obeying God's commands. Sacrifice has to be coupled with a trust that God will provide and protect us in all situations and circumstances. We have to trust that our sacrifice is in keeping with His will for us. However, sacrifice alone is not what God wants from us. In Psalm 4:5 (NIV) we're told to, "Offer right sacrifices and trust in the Lord." One of the best examples of blessings we will receive when we trust in the Lord is written in Jeremiah 17:5-7 (NIV). Jeremiah wrote,

> This is what the Lord says: Cursed is the one who trusts in man, who depends on flesh for his strength and whose heart turns away from the Lord. He will be like a bush in the wastelands; he will not see prosperity when it comes. He will dwell in the parched places of the desert, in a salt land where no one lives.
>
> But blessed is the man who trusts in the Lord, whose confidence is in him. He will be like a tree planted by the water that sends out its roots by the stream. It does not fear when heat comes; its leaves are always green. It has no worries in a year of drought and never fails to bear fruit.

I attempted to be cautious in selecting people to profile in this chapter. In most cases I had to rely on their own words and actions in discerning whether their trust was in self or in the Lord, and to trust that the Holy Spirit would guide me in that discernment. For instance, one of the people I considered profiling was a sports figure who sacrificed a lucrative career to serve in the US Army. I was moved by his sacrifice, but he acknowledged he didn't have a relationship with God, and didn't believe in Him. He didn't lose his life because he didn't trust in the Lord, but his *life* was lost because he didn't trust in the Lord.

Alvin York will be profiled a little later in this chapter, but he is being introduced now because he exemplifies the transformation of a person professing a life of sin and shunning of God's grace to a person fully trusting in the Lord as he wrestled with the decision to sacrifice for his country and the many people he would never know. An entry in his diary from October 5, 1918 reads,

> Argonne Forest, France-- We went out on the main road and lined up and started for the front and the Germans was shelling the road and the airplanes was humming over our heads, and we were stumbling over dead horses and dead men, and the shells were bursting all around us. And then it was I could see the power of God helped men if they would only trust Him.
> Oh, it was there I could look up and say:
>> "O Jesus, the great rock of foundation
>> Whereon my feet were set with sovereign grace.
>> Through shells or death with all their agitation.
>> Thou wilt protect me if I will only trust in Thy grace.
>> Bless Thy Holy Name!"

'When thou goest out to battle against thine enemies, and seest horses, and chariots, and a people more than thou, be not afraid of them: for the LORD thy God is with thee, which brought thee up out of the land of Egypt.
~ Deuteronomy 20:1 ~
(Diary of Alvin York, 2010)

Common definitions of a Christian are being a "little Christ" or like Christ. What a wonderful association to be pegged with. However, to be like Christ requires a person to emulate more than selflessness through good works or even selflessness coupled with sacrifice, or caring, or discipleship for that matter. Each Christ-like attribute should be viewed as a single link in a chain. The links of a chain are dependent on each other for strength and to be able to perform the tasks required of the chain. A single link has little flexibility and, except for hanging keys on it, it has even less purpose. Adding another link creates some flexibility in the chain, but its purpose is still limited. A third and fourth link create more flexibility, and the end links can be connected to each other to 'close the loop', so to speak. But, it isn't until the chain has five or more links that it can begin to take the shape resembling the crown of thorns that adorned Christ's head as he hung on the Cross, or the crown that will become our reward when we are gathered into His presence. God will not be impressed by the size of anyone's crown, but it won't rest squarely on the head if it only has one or two links, unless nails from the Cross are used to hold it in place.

Sacrifice is most often associated with death, and many of the people profiled in this chapter did sacrifice their life for someone they didn't know or maybe even for generations of unknown people. It's unfortunate that we relate sacrifice and death together because, as I mentioned earlier, sacrifice can also mean giving up some material thing or future opportunity in exchange for something else. The ultimate sacrifice was made by God when he offered his Son as atonement for the sin of the world. Jesus paid the price, but it was God who offered the sacrifice.

September 11, 2001, was a day when many invisible heroes where at work. I chose one who will likely be familiar to most readers to exemplify the sacrifice for the many on that day. His name is Todd Beamer. Based on what I have come to know about Todd, I'm sure he would be uncomfortable having the spotlight shine on him personally. Rather he would like to simply be remembered as a 'go-to' person who was in a position to exemplify Christ Jesus to his fellow passengers on United Flight 93, and will continue to be a witness to future generations. He had been walking in Jesus' footsteps since he accepted Him as his Savior at age seven, so his natural reaction to the situation unfolding around him was to seek God's guidance and trust that whatever happened was in keeping with His will.

Todd's wife, Lisa, wrote in *Let's Roll!,* "Todd wanted his life to count; he wanted to *live* the Christian life, not just talk about it. While many of Todd's college classmates went into ministerial professions, Todd felt that he didn't need to be a 'professional' preacher to serve God. He could serve God in business as well – and maybe even make more of an impact on the world than he could by speaking from a pulpit. Although his close friends and family members didn't understand all that Todd meant at the time, one day they would … and in a way the go-to guy himself would never have guessed" (p. 31 – 32).

One way that Todd has impacted my life has been through Lisa's book. That might seem like a stretch, but if Todd and his fellow passengers hadn't sacrificed their lives on that day, Lisa wouldn't have written her book and I wouldn't have learned about another invisible hero whose footsteps lead to the Cross.

Lisa tells of her own heroes, invisible to us and to the world outside of Peekskill, NY, but very visible to her as she grappled with the passing of her father when she was 15. The heroes that continued to lead her to the Cross as she questioned her commitment to Christ with all of the "why?" questions following the loss of a loved one included Dennis Massaro, and Joe and Karen Urbanowicz (p. 82 – 86). I don't know anything more about them than what Lisa details in her book, but I wanted to share that with you to reinforce my earlier assertion that we all have heroes around us whose footsteps can lead us to the Cross or keep us moving along Christ's pathway if we will only take time to narrow our field of vision, and focus on the meaningful attributes that we should be emulating.

Another way Todd impacted the world on September 11 didn't have anything to do with acts of bravery, but instead was in how he witnessed to others. The November 26, 2001, issue of Newsweek contains an article by Karen Breslau, Eleanor Clift and Evan Thomas detailing the conversation Todd had with Lisa Jefferson, GTE supervisor. The article states:

> Up to this moment, Beamer had been all business.
> "Lisa," he said suddenly. "Yes?" responded
> Jefferson. "That's my wife," said Beamer. "Well,
> that's my name, too, Todd," said Jefferson. "Oh,

my God," said Beamer. "I don't think we're going to get out of this thing. I'm going to have to go out on faith." Jefferson tried to comfort him. "Todd," she said, "you don't know that." Beamer asked her to promise to call his wife if he didn't make it home. He told her about his little boys and the new baby on the way. Then he said that the passengers were going to try to jump the hijackers. "Are you sure that's what you want to do, Todd?" asked Jefferson. "It's what we have to do," he answered. He asked her to pray with him. Beamer kept a Lord's Prayer bookmark in his Tom Clancy novel, but he didn't need any prompting. He began to recite the ancient litany, and she joined him:

> Our Father which art in heaven, Hallowed be thy name. Thy kingdom come. Thy will be done in earth, as it is in heaven. Give us this day our daily bread. And forgive us our trespasses, as we forgive those who trespass against us. And lead us not into temptation, but deliver us from evil: For thine is the kingdom, and the power, and the glory, for ever. Amen.

Later, just before the passengers attempted to regain control of the airplane, Todd recited one of the most comforting prayers of the Bible, the 23rd Psalm.

> The Lord is my shepherd, I shall not be in want. He makes me lie down in green pastures, he leads me beside quiet waters, he restores my soul. He guides me in paths of righteousness for his name's sake. Even though I walk through the valley of the shadow of death, I will fear no evil, for you are with me; your rod and your staff, they comfort me. You prepare a table before me in the presence of my enemies. You anoint my head with oil; my cup overflows. Surely goodness and love will

> follow me all the days of my life, and I will dwell in the house of the Lord forever. (NIV) (Breslau, et al, 2001).

A few weeks after Todd's death, Lisa was going through some papers in his office when she found a quote by Theodore Roosevelt in his in-box. The quote reads:

> The credit belongs to the man who is actually in the arena…who strives valiantly, who knows the great enthusiasms, the great devotions, and spends himself in worthy causes. Who, at best, knows the triumph of high achievement and who, at worst, if he fails, fails while daring greatly so that his place shall never be with those cold and timid souls who know neither victory or defeat (Breslau, et al, 2001).

I can't help but believe that Todd is enjoying the victory that comes through a life dedicated to Christ Jesus. There were many invisible heroes in Todd's life and now he continues to be an invisible hero to all those who come to know how he lived his life and walked in the footsteps of Jesus.

As I was doing my research, I felt the Holy Spirit guiding me along the way. Almost daily I would be directed to another person or reminded of a situation that I needed to investigate. I don't know how Todd Beamer came into mind, except by the Holy Spirit of course, but I do know why. In an early chapter of *Let's Roll!*, Lisa comments that Todd attended Wheaton College, which is also the alma mater of several other "invisible heroes" including Billy Graham, former Speaker of the House, Dennis Hastert, and the martyred missionary, Jim Elliot (p. 19). I didn't remember who Jim Elliot was, but I would soon find out as the Holy Spirit guided me to look into the details of a movie I had seen some time earlier titled *End of the Spear.*

That movie stirred me emotionally, but I didn't know any of the background. When I started this chapter I had to ask my wife to refresh my memory of the name of the movie because I wanted to find out more about the pilot. My online search revealed the pilot's name was Nate Saint.

Lisa's reference to Jim Elliot caused me to stop and investigate him further also. To my naïve surprise, not only did Jim Elliot attend Wheaton College, but Nate Saint, and Ed Mc Cully did as well; and furthermore they all died spreading God's Word in the remotest parts of the Amazon jungle. I wonder if Todd was conscious of the footsteps he was following when he decided to attend Wheaton.

The lives of those martyred missionaries, their families, and the Huaorani people are so intertwined that I can't profile one without profiling them all. They have all sacrificed while following the Great Commission that Jesus charged the eleven, and all of us as well, to undertake. He said, "All authority in heaven and on earth has been given to me. Therefore go and make disciples of all nations, baptizing them in the name of the Father and of the Son and of the Holy Spirit, and teaching them to obey everything I have commanded you. And surely I am with you always, to the very end of the age" (Mt. 28:18b-20 NIV). The missionaries lived and died carrying out that commission.

Nate's son, Steve, was five at the time of his father's death. He didn't know why the men died, but he knew his father and the other men were not afraid to face the unknown and that they were determined to go where the Holy Spirit lead them. All of the adult family members felt the same calling. In fact, Steve's aunt, Rachel Saint, and Jim Elliot's wife, Elisabeth, ventured into the jungle to live with the same Huaorani people, practice basic medicine for them, and study the language so they could some day translate the Bible and share God's Word with the people. Steve spent many summers with the women and came to learn the Huaorani customs and culture. However, he didn't question any of the men of the tribe about the details of the murders until a visit in the 1990s. Here is part of that story as told by Steve in his book *End of the Spear,* an article titled "Did They Have to Die?" in *Christianity Today.* Both were summarized under the *Christianity Today* title at http://www.atanycost.org, which is the resource quoted.

In January, 1956, after a number of contacts with the Huaorani people, missionaries Nate Saint, Jim Elliot, Ed McCully, Pete

Fleming, and Roger Youderian set up camp on a little sandbar near the tribe's jungle village hoping to make contact. Steve writes:

> The group wanted to make contact with the primitive Aucas, known for their fierce infighting and hatred of outsiders. The five missionaries had a deep burden to share the gospel message with a people known only for hunting and killing. Their initial friendly contact ended in death by spearing.
>
> So much was the same (40 years later), and yet circumstances were so different! The past three weeks I had been carving a new airstrip out of the virgin jungle with "the people" (which is what their own Huaorani word means), some of whom had murdered my father and his friends just before my fifth birthday. Mincaye was one of them. Mincaye, with whom I had just gone hunting, who laughed and joked about everything, who had tried the hula hoop on his first friendly contact with the outside. He had been on the beach that fateful day in 1956. There was no laughing on that visit.
> Dyuwi, shy, sweet Dyuwi, who hung around our camp each night waiting for a break in the conversation so he could thank Wangongi (creator God) for keeping us safe from falling trees, Konga ants, and poisonous snakes: he too had been there. Just a teenager then, and certainly just as shy, he was nevertheless an up-and-coming killer who knew what they had come to do and went about it- no doubt with the same vigor I had seen him demonstrate on a huge stump he'd been working for the last three days to clear from our landing strip.
> Kimo, who brought his canoe full of provisions so we would have plenty to eat while we worked on the strip, had also been there in 1956. He told me that the last of the five young cowodi

(foreigners/strangers) had fled across the river, away from the attack, and instead of fleeing into the jungle and safety, had climbed onto a log and called in poor Huao, 'We just came to meet you. We aren't going to hurt you. Why are you killing us?' It was this same gentle Kimo who listened to this plea and then ran a nine-foot hardwood spear through the foreigner's chest.

Why did these gentle, kindhearted men I had been eating, sleeping, and working alongside kill my father and his friends? Why did the missionaries not defend themselves with guns against primitive spears?

Nate Saint, Jim Elliot, and Ed McCully, three college friends working as missionaries in Ecuador, had a burning desire to follow Jesus' command to take the gospel message into all the world. They had prayed for years for this primitive group that had never heard the redemption story of peace with God through the death of Christ.

These five men were not cast from the same mold. Jim was impetuous but focused. Both a college wrestler and a writer, his good looks and physical strength were matched by a deep introspection. Ed McCully, president of his college class, had played football end and won his senior oratory contest. Everyone expected him to go to law school, but something stronger called him to the jungles of the Amazon. Dad was born into an artist's family but picked up a stray gene. He loved the technical and mechanical aspects of life and wanted to use his interest and skills for a purpose with dimensions that would honor God and outlast the temporal. Flying support for missionaries was a way to fulfill both of his desires. Pete was the youngest of the group, but in some ways the group's sage. Roger was the guy you sent to do the job when it took dogged determination and a completely willing heart to get it done.

Here were five common young men whose unifying distinction was less their inherited abilities or acquired skills than their commitment to seek God's will and to carry out his purposes for their lives. They were aware of the risk they were taking but felt it was justified, though they could have had no idea of the impact their martyrdom would someday have.

They [the missionaries] gleaned a short repertoire of Huao phrases from Dayuma, a Huao girl who had fled almost certain death from intratribal spearings and was living on a hacienda outside Huao territory. My father's sister, Rachel, was living with Dayuma and studying the Huao language, sure that God had called her to live with this tribe someday and teach them how to walk on God's trail.

The missionaries began making regular overflights to drop friendship gifts from the plane, calling over a loudspeaker, 'We like you. We are your friends.' Soon they decided to try the bucket drop, a technique Dad had developed to deliver and retrieve items from missionaries who had no airstrip. He circled his plane overhead in tight circles while a long cord with the goods attached was reeled out behind the plane.

The Huaorani tell me that when this technique was used, they understood that the gifts were being deliberately offered and signaled their understanding and desire to continue the exchange by tying on gifts of their own. They remember receiving machetes, a metal axe (a prized possession among people who traditionally used stone axes), brightly colored ribbons, and aluminum cooking pots. In exchange, they returned a Huao comb, a feather headdress, smoked monkey, and even a live parrot, which became my childhood pet.

On January 2, 1956, Dad flew the four other men in one by one, and they set up camp on what they called "Palm Beach." They made repeated flights back and forth to the Huaorani settlement so that the people would figure out that the plane was no longer flying off into the distance but landing in their territory.

After three days of waiting on the beach, the men suddenly saw two naked women step out of the jungle onto the opposite bank. Two missionaries waded out into the river to greet them. When it was apparent the women were being well received, a man joined them on the beach. Dad's journal records that the three Huaorani seemed relaxed and acted in a friendly manner. They shared the missionaries' hamburgers and Koolaid and carried on an animated conversation as if their every word were understood. The man, whom the missionaries nicknamed "George," made it obvious that he understood the men had arrived in the ibo (Huao for woodbee or airplane) and he wanted a ride. Dad took him for a quick spin, which wasn't enough, and then for a second ride over his settlement, where his people saw him in the plane .

The next day there were no visitors, but in an overflight on January 8, Dad spotted a party of ten Huaorani on their way to the beach. (The jungle growth is too thick to be able to see the trail, so this chance spotting probably occurred as the group crossed the Tiwaeno River.) At noon, Dad radioed to my mother. 'Looks like they'll be here for the Sunday afternoon service. This is it! Pray for us. Will contact you again at 4:30, over and out.' As soon as 4:30 came without word from the always punctual Nate, Mom knew something was wrong and contacted the other missionary pilot. He flew over the beach the next morning, spotting the plane stripped of its canvas covering and one body in the river. Four days later a weary but tense ground party made up of missionaries, Quechua Indians, and military personnel found the other bodies, identifiable only by their watches, rings, and other personal effects. Photos developed from film found in Dad's camera at the bottom of the river, a diary fished out of his pocket, and his watch, stopped at 3:10, seemed to be all there was to tell about the end of his life.

After the murders, my Aunt Rachel continued learning the Huao language, taking the apostle Paul's words as a personal promise. 'Those who were not told will see, and those who have not heard will understand.' Dayuma also believed the words Rachel taught her from the Bible and decided to return to her people, to teach them what she had learned about God and the outside world of the cowodi. Less than three years after the massacre, Aunt Rachel and Jim Elliot's widow, Elisabeth, had made contact and were living among the tribe. There they practiced basic medicine and began to notate an oral language in hopes of someday translating the Scriptures into Huao-tidido (the Huao language) (At Any Cost, 2003).

Steve continues,
> Though I knew which men had killed Dad, it was not something I asked about.

But finally, last year, during my most recent journey to build a new airstrip and clinic with the Huaorani, I asked the evangelist Dyuwi how many times he had killed before he began to walk on God's trail as a young man. We were sitting outside Dayuma's house in the village of Tonampade, named after one of my childhood friends, Tona. He became the first Huao martyr, speared while trying to reach his downriver relatives with the gospel. I sat in the shade with Dyuwi and others, some of us swinging in hammocks and some squatting by an open groundfire. Children played nearby with clipped-winged birds. In a rush of stories, Dyuwi, Kimo, Dawa, Gikita, and Mincaye, all participants that day on the beach, paid me a high compliment by speaking openly of the killing. They knew that all of us have experienced God's forgiveness and that they had nothing to fear from me.

As they described their recollections, it occurred to me how incredibly unlikely it was that the Palm Beach killing took place at all; it is an anomaly that I cannot explain outside of divine intervention.

The Huaorani killed for various reasons: revenge, anger, frustration, fear. Sometimes it took very little provocation. But they always wanted two things: superiority of force and surprise. In contemplating an attack on Palm Beach, they knew they would not have a superior force. Six men with spears was hardly a match for five likely armed cowodi. If they killed the cowodi they knew they would have to burn their houses, leave their gardens, and flee as they always did after attacks, because they knew that other cowodi would come in their ibos and find them. Add to this the fact that five of the six attackers were just teenagers, not

> seasoned killers, and that one witness to the Friday contact insisted the cowodi were friendly. Under these circumstances, it seems hard to believe there ever was an attack; yet there was.
>
> On Sunday afternoon, when the killers finally arrived at Palm Beach, they could see that there were five cowodi, and that they had guns. We know that the guns, which were primarily intended for protection from animals, were usually kept out of sight. The missionaries had vowed to one another before God that they would not defend themselves against human attack, even in the face of death (At Any Cost, 2003).

The missionaries were true to their word and didn't resist the attack. God had placed them in that situation for a purpose that wouldn't be revealed until Rachel, Elisabeth, and Dayuma went to live with the people and teach them the Word. All of the participants in the killings have made profession of faith, been baptized, and welcomed into God's family. God's saving grace has been imparted upon many as the result of the sacrifice of a few who dared to accept the Great Commission.

Sacrifice and the service of uniformed men and women are not an uncommon duo. Most people have the perception that donning a uniform symbolizes a willingness to step into harm's way and make the ultimate sacrifice for a fellow service member or a person that uniformed personnel have taken an oath to protect. That may certainly be true for many, and is probably the case for career personnel, but for some there are a number of other reasons. In my case, my initial entry into the military was all about self. The Army meant a job, a ticket away from my hometown, an opportunity for travel and adventure, a chance to gain a better understanding of what I really wanted to do with my life, and a number of other reasons. When all was said and done I served 26 years of combined active, National Guard, and Army Reserve duty over a 33 year period with occasional breaks to focus on family, civilian career, and to take a breather. I served in Vietnam early in my career and in Desert Storm towards the end of my career. One might conclude that I made a number of sacrifices for family, country, fellow soldiers, and strangers in foreign lands. However, it wasn't until late in my career that I really understood my own motivation. Self was always part of the equation as I aspired to earn medals and other accolades, admiration, and retirement security, but as many men and women who serve come to realize, Christ called us all to serve one another with the gifts and talents that He blessed us with. When I recognized that calling I realigned my motivation to match God's will and my service took on a new meaning.

Since this book is not about me I don't want to spend much time there. The example of my uniformed service was intended to lead into the profiles of a few men far more deserving than me. Serving others ahead of self always requires sacrifice because we are required to give up something for someone or something else.

There is so much to share about Sgt. Alvin York (1887 – 1964). It's unfortunate that space constrains my ambition to tell his whole story. Perhaps I can profile him again in a future edition. As I referenced earlier, Sgt. York kept a diary of his service in World War I. The diary covers the period from the time he received the first letter to register for the draft until he retuned home in 1919. All of the quotes are from his diary. Additional diary entries and a short story about his life can be found at http://acacia.pair.com/Acacia.Vignettes/The.Diary.of.Alvin.York.html.

Alvin was raised in a Christian home, but he fought God as hard as he fought friends and strangers alike when he was drinking moonshine and gambling away his earnings. His mother was patient and persistent in her requests for him to reform his ways. As the story goes, Alvin was brawling one night and a friend was killed. That incident didn't change his life, but it was a wake-up call. He tells how he came home one night from drinking and fighting to find his mother waiting up for him. In his words,

> I got in after midnight, and found my mother sitting up waiting for me, and I asked her, 'Why don't you lie down?' And she said, 'I can't lie down. I don't know what's going to become of you when you are out drinking, and so I wait until you

> come in.' And then she asked me, 'Alvin, when are you going to be a man like your father and your grandfathers?' I promised my mother that night I would never drink again; I would never smoke or chew again; I would never gamble again; I would never cuss or fight again. And I have never drunk any whiskey, I have never touched cards, I have never smoked or chewed, and I have never fought or rough-housed since that night. I was very fond of tobacco, too. I used to smoke and chew. And there was plenty of cheap whisky. You could always get it. And I was big and hard, over six feet and weighed upwards of 180 pounds. And when I quit, I quit all. I am very glad I did. I am a good deal like Paul, the things I once loved, I now hate (Diary of Alvin York, 2010).

His conversion came shortly after that. He says he was 29 when he accepted the Lord as his Savior. Alvin had a couple of invisible heroes in his life too. Besides the examples of his mother and father, there were two other strong influences in his life, Rev. M.H. Russell, an evangelist from Indiana, and Pastor Pile, the preacher at Alvin's local church. He remarked about the influence of Rev. Russell as,

> He was an evangelist who preached very close. All that was not right he fought. He had a wonderful meeting there. He had more conversions than any one man that has ever been through the valley. Well, the way he impressed me was by his true speaking of the Scriptures. I knew the Scriptures, and when he spoke from them he spoke truly, giving the punishment for the wicked and the place of happiness for those who are in Christ Jesus (Diary of Alvin York, 2010).

The story of his sacrifice to protect the lives of the people around him during the battle of the Argonne Forest in October 1918 is not as much a story of *his* deeds as it a story of God's protection. After the

Armistice was signed, General Lindsay asked York to describe the events of the battle. York replied,

> Sir, it is not man power. A higher power than man power guided and watched over me and told me what to do. And the general bowed his head and put his hand on my shoulder and solemnly said, 'York, you are right.'
> There can be no doubt in the world of the fact of the divine power being in that. No other power under heaven could bring a man out of a place like that. Men were killed on both sides of me; and I was the biggest and the most exposed of all. Over thirty machine guns were maintaining rapid fire at me, point-blank from a range of about twenty-five yards (Diary of Alvin York, 2010).

Like Todd Beamer, Sgt. York took comfort in knowing that God was with him at all times and that He would not lay a burden on him that couldn't be handled if he trusted that the Lord would carry him through. One of Alvin's comforting verses was, "The LORD is my rock, and my fortress, and my deliverer; my God, my strength, in whom I will trust; my buckler, and the horn of my salvation, and my high tower" (Psalm 18:2 KJV).

Time of Reflection

Read Psalm 4:5, 18:2, and Jeremiah 17:5-7 and discuss the following questions.

- When faced with uncertainty, where does God want us to turn for help?
- When things aren't going well, what do you cling to for strength?
- David called God his "rock", in whom he took refuge. How is God a refuge in your life?
- How will God respond to people who put their trust in things of this world?

Integrity/Character

"May integrity and uprightness protect me,
because my hope is in you."
- Psalm 25:21 (NIV)

The Merriam-Webster dictionary defines character as, "moral excellence and firmness," and integrity as, "firm adherence to a code of especially moral or artistic values." In David's prayer above he prays that God will enable him to live a moral life through his trust in Him. This chapter will profile others whose life characterizes David's prayer, even when doing so could be detrimental to their career or ambitions in the secular world we live in.

Integrity and character could be two separate links in the chain of a Christ-centered life, or they can be combined into a single link. I have combined them in this chapter because of the thin line of distinction between them. In Romans, Paul says, "…but we also rejoice in our suffering, because we know that suffering produces perseverance; perseverance, character; and character, hope" (Ro 5:3b-4 NIV). In 1 Kings 9:4-6 (NIV), God tells Solomon, "As for you, if you walk before me in integrity of heart and uprightness, as David your father did, and do all I command and observe my decrees and laws, I will establish your royal throne over Israel forever, as I promised David your father…"

It was hard for both David and Solomon to maintain their character and integrity in spite of their closeness to God and His favor upon them. That is not untypical of public figures today. Some public figures don't try to hide their contempt for God's commands while others try to live in two worlds – one the public sees and one that comes out behind closed doors. I was disappointed to find so many living in the latter example.

When did it become politically incorrect to be a Christian in the United States? Just as there was no room in the inn for Jesus to be born, there seems to be no room in politics for Him now. If Samuel Adams (1722 – 1803) represents the character and integrity of our forefathers, then we have drifted far from the path they set us on. Following the signing of the Declaration of Independence, Samuel Adams declared, "We have this day restored the Sovereign to whom alone men ought to be obedient. He reigns in Heaven, and with a propitious eye beholds his subjects assuming that freedom of thought and dignity of self-direction which He bestowed on them. From the rising to the setting sun, may His kingdom come!" (Samuel Adams Quotes, 2010). Samuel Adams put great stock in the right character of public figures. In a letter to James Warren dated November 4, 1775, Adams stated, "Nothing is more essential to the establishment of manners in a State than that all persons employed in places of power and trust be men of unexceptionable characters. The public cannot be too curious concerning the character of public men" (Samuel Adams Quotes, 2010). Rick Warren echoed that charge when he said, "Whether leading in business, education, politics, or family, character always trumps charisma. What we desperately need in our leaders today is character" (Warren, 2008). It seems that the public, in general, isn't curious enough any more to ensure only people of great character are afforded the opportunity and privilege of governing others. Integrity and character have taken a backseat to the quest for power, financial gain, and control.

Fortunately, there are still some people of integrity and character in the public realm who follow in Christ's footsteps and are willing to publically proclaim their faith and hold themselves open for scrutiny. One such person is Dan Quayle.

For those who don't remember Dan Quayle, he was Vice President during the senior George Bush administration. The media made sport of Vice President Quayle and seemed to work tirelessly to find even one skeleton in his closet during the campaign and his term in office. They were never successful in finding one. In his book, *Standing Firm,* VP Quayle notes how he and his wife, Marilyn, drew much of their strength from people who would testify to their own faith and encourage the Quayles with their prayers. Vice Presidet Quayle said, "It was tremendous, because I believe in the power of prayer. Marilyn and I pray every day, not just in crises like this one [the presidential campaign], because faith has to be more than a crutch and more than an emergency measure" (p. 53). He tells about one situation where his and Marilyn's faith, strength, integrity, and character were all put to the test during a TV interview between Jane Pauley and Marilyn. He wrote, "[Jane] asked Marilyn a question about her supposedly far-out religious beliefs and her father's faith. Marilyn looked shocked and said, 'My father is a wonderful gentleman, he has nothing to do with Dan's campaign. I don't understand any of this. I'm a Presbyterian. I go to Fourth Presbyterian Church. I really didn't know that wasn't acceptable'" (p. 57). He went on to point out, "Christianity is central to our lives, but to many in the media and the entertainment industry, Christianity is something that consists chiefly of corrupt televangelists and 'redneck' rabblerousing, something to be cartooned and ridiculed" (p.57)

He sums up his faith and trust in Jesus as his Savior as, "My faith in God and belief in the Bible is an important part of my life but nothing for others to fear. Faith in God is personal and cannot be mandated by a government. Our pastors lead us and help us to understand the Word, but the Bible always remains, eternal and unchangeable. Its words would be my solace and strength in the weeks and years ahead" (p.58)

Public testament to one's faith is difficult for some to discuss because it isn't "politically correct." Supposedly a public figure should be neutral when it comes to professing his/her faith, especially if the person happens to be Christian. On the other hand, there are people who openly profess their faith, but their actions demonstrate otherwise. Maybe dogged media scrutiny has something to do with Christians in the public arena shying away from public profession of their faith.

There is a new face on the national scene that isn't afraid to step out in faith and open herself up to scrutiny by the media. That person is Sarah Palin. Once in a while a person comes into the public spotlight emitting a glow and freshness that causes others to believe that the vision of our founding fathers is still alive and well. Public figures are usually stiff and inaccessible. Referring to a public figure by his or her first name seems clumsy because that is an honor afforded to only a few select "inner circle" people. However, referring to Gov. Sarah Palin in any way other than "Sarah" just doesn't seem right. She's comfortable with getting up-close and personal and wants others to feel the same towards her. My wife, Pat, attended a book signing for Sarah's, *Going Rogue – An American Life,* shortly after the book came out and had the opportunity to chat with her. People in the signing line had been told that Sarah wouldn't have time to meet and greet everyone, but it turned out exactly the opposite. Sarah took time to shake hands with everyone and personalize a conversation. In Pat's case, Sarah noticed that she was wearing an Alaska sweatshirt so she had to ask if Pat had been there, where she visited, the circumstances for the visit, etc. Pat was embarrassed and honored by the attention. Sarah doesn't know us, but we feel we know her. I believe her comfort level stems from the physical and family environment that she grew up in.

Having been raised in the Midwest where crime, drugs, alcohol abuse, racism, and competition to climb the ladder of success were not a part of my life, I can empathize with Sarah. Maybe that's why she is so popular with the common people who continue to make this country as great as it is in spite of Washington Beltway politics.

John Adams said, "Because power corrupts, society's demands for moral authority and character increase as the importance of the position increases" (John Adams, 2010). As a powerful political figure, Sarah Palin is very aware of the truth of John Adams' words. In *Sarah Palin – A New Kind of Leader,* (Zondervan, 2008) Joseph Hilley writes,

> At the center of Sarah Palin's moral core lies a profound belief in God, the Judeo-Christian God of Abraham, Isaac, and Jacob who is more fully revealed in the person and work of Jesus Christ. That belief arises from Sarah's personal spiritual insight, but it encompasses three main themes that inform all others: (1) a commitment to the truth and authority of Scriptures, (2) a keen sense of justice, and (3) an ethic of personal responsibility.
>
> For Sarah, the Bible is not merely a book, but a record of God's revelation to humanity (p. 69-70).

It is widely known that Sarah is the mother of a child with Down Syndrome. When the doctor told her that tests had revealed the child's developmental disorder, there was no question as to what her decision would be. She trusted that God would provide the strength necessary to raise her son in a loving, Christ-centered home, and that he would bring great joy to Sarah and her family.

In a magazine totally devoted to Sarah titled, *Sarah Palin – The Untold Story…in her own words!,* she shares an interview with Katie Couric that was recorded during the 2008 presidential campaign. Sarah wrote, "She asked me 12 different times my position on abortion and the morning-after pill. She did not, I guess, want to hear my first, candid truthful response about being pro-life. I think she was out to get anyone who didn't believe in her perspective" (p. 80). I admire Sarah for sharing her faith so openly and for being so tenacious in not succumbing to media pressure for her to acquiesce.

Gov. Mike Huckabee makes no bones about where he stands in his walk with Christ Jesus either. Mike was a pastor for 12 years, Lt. Governor of Arkansas for three years, and Governor of Arkansas for ten years. Although the responsibilities of the man changed, the convictions of the man were steadfast. He is steadfast in his position on Biblical inerrancy, which holds that once a man disregards the ultimate truthfulness of the Bible, then anything can become justifiable. Gov. Huckabee leaves no doubt where he stands on abortion, embryonic stem-cell research, and same-sex marriage. However, he doesn't believe the federal government should be in a position of legislating morality. Government leadership should surely influence Christian values through their own example and testimony, but he asserts, as he wrote in *Do the Right Thing,* "To force a religious belief on another – insofar as that's even possible – violates the most basic concept of the Judeo-Christian worldview that God loves us out of His own volition and seeks a relationship with us. A relationship can be valid only when all parties agree to it" (p. 50). He also expressed that, "Faith (or the lack of it, for that matter) frames who we are, what we think, and how we approach issues and problems. Our own faith gives us the road map for the way we live, but does not mean we own the whole road and can drive on it without respect for the designated lanes, other drivers, or signs" (p.51).

Gov. Huckabee is not shy about his love for the Lord and his desire to follow in His footsteps. What is needed in the United States today are leaders who can provide the moral guidance necessary to lead our country back to the vision that Samuel Adams and the other founders had when they gave birth to this great nation. Mike Huckabee, Sarah Palin, and Dan Quayle are examples of that kind of leadership. But instead of following their examples, we are being governed and lead by people who are only concerned about self and perpetuating their own political futures. As a nation we are teetering on the brink of destruction just as Judah and the people of Jerusalem were in the time of the prophet Jeremiah. Substitute "people of the United States" for "people of Judah" and "Washington, DC" for "Jerusalem" in these passages from Jeremiah and see the path we are on.

> This is the word that came to Jeremiah from the Lord: Listen to the terms of this covenant and tell them to the people of [United States] and to those who live in [Washington, DC]. Tell them that this is what the Lord, the God of Israel says: 'Cursed is the man who does not obey the terms of this covenant – the terms I commanded your forefathers when I brought them out of Egypt, out of the iron-smelting furnace.' I said, 'Obey me and do everything I command you, and you will be my people and I will be your God. Then I will fulfill the oath I swore to your forefathers, to give them a land flowing with milk and honey' – the land you possess today (Jeremiah 11:1-5a NIV).

> 'There is a conspiracy among the people of [United States] and those who live in [Washington, DC]. They have returned to the sins of their forefathers, who refused to listen to my words. They have followed other gods to serve them. Both the house of Israel and the house of [United States] have broken the covenant I made with their forefathers. Therefore this is what the Lord says: 'I will bring on them a disaster they cannot escape. Although they cry out to me, I will not listen to them. The towns of [United States] and the people of [Washington, DC] will go and cry out to the

gods to whom they burn incense, but they will not help them at all when disaster strikes. You have as many gods as you have towns, O [United States]; and the altars you have set up to burn incense to that shameful god Baal are as many as the streets of [Washington, DC]' (Jeremiah 11:9b-13 NIV).

No matter where Dan, Sarah, or Mike go in their political careers, God will be there too, because they have come to know and trust God's promise that He will always be with those who obey His commands. The United States needs leaders of integrity or we shall surely be overwhelmed and subdued by the angels of Satan that are already chiseling away at our Christian foundation.

John McCain rounds out a trio of Christ-focused political leaders who were foes, running mates, and friends during the 2008 presidential campaign. John McCain could easily have been profiled in the chapter on sacrifice, but I thought it would be more fitting to include him with his colleagues as another example of the integrity that is still alive and well in at least some part of politics. John McCain was a real Vietnam hero, not as much for his exploits as for the character and integrity he demonstrated during the 5 1/2 years he was a prisoner-of-war.

Senator McCain experienced strain on his love for Christ and his country beyond what we can comprehend. He shared part of that strain in his book, *Faith of My Fathers.* He wrote,

> During our worst moments of captivity, keeping our faith in God, country, and one another was as difficult as it was imperative. When your faith weakened, you had to take any opportunity, seize on any sight of it, and use any temporary relief from your distress to recover it.
> POWs often regard their prison experience as comparable to the trials of Job. Indeed, for my fellow prisoners who suffered more than I, the comparison is appropriate. Hungry, beaten, hurt, scared, and alone, human beings can begin to feel that they are removed from God's love, a vast

> distance separating them from their Creator. The anguish can lead to resentment, to the awful despair that God has forsaken you.
>
> To guard against such despair, in our most dire moments, POWs would make supreme efforts to grasp our faith tightly, to profess it alone, in the dark, and hasten its revival. Once I was thrown into another cell after a long and difficult interrogation. I discovered scratched into one of the cell's walls the creed "I believe in God, the Father Almighty." There, standing witness to God's presence in a remote, concealed place, recalled to my faith by a stronger, better man, I felt God's love and care more vividly than I would have felt it had I been safe among a pious congregation in the most magnificent cathedral (p. 253-254).

Sen. McCain also wrote about the strength that sustained him during that difficult time and the strength that continues to sustain him as he deals with the challenges of being a Christian in the Gomorrah-like capital of the United States. In his words,

> My first concern was not that I might fail God and country, although I certainly hoped that I would not. I was afraid to fail my friends. I was afraid to come back from an interrogation and tell them I couldn't hold up as well as they had. However I measured my character before Vietnam no longer mattered. What mattered now was how they measured my character. My self-regard became indivisible from their regard for me. And it will remain so for the rest of my life (p. 256).

Living a life for Christ and leaving footsteps to the Cross for others to follow is about as difficult in the sports and entertainment businesses as it is in the political arena, but that doesn't mean that we are void of examples to follow. One example is Ernie Harwell (1918 -) the broadcast voice of the Detroit Tigers for 42 years.

I don't know if people tuned in to Ernie to follow the Tigers or just to listen to his play-by-play of the game. He could certainly captivate an audience. Ernie started every new season by reading from the Song of Solomon 2:11-12 (KJV), "For lo, the winter is past, the rain is over and gone; the flowers appear on the earth; the time of the singing of birds is come, and the voice of the turtle is heard in our land" (*Ernie Harwell:* Wikipedia, 2010). No one seemed to question whether it was appropriate to read from the Bible at the beginning of a baseball season, but everyone ***expected*** Ernie to do it. Stepping out boldly in faith was part of what Ernie was all about, and what an important part it was.

Ernie turned his life over to Christ in 1961 after attending one of Billy Graham's crusades in Florida and he never looked back. In an interview with Mitch Albom in the fall of 2009, Ernie talked about his inoperable cancer and the comfort he has knowing that Christ Jesus is walking along side of him through the final journey of his life. He said, "I don't know how many days I've got left, but I praise God because he's given me this time. I can really know whose arms I'm going to end up in, and what a great, great thing heaven is going to be" (Albom, 2009).

Ernie has spent most of his life bringing joy to baseball fans of all ages and an equal time in his own joy of knowing that God has been by his side all that time. Ernie has never hesitated to praise God for his blessings. Maybe there are a number of Ernie's fans who are following in his footsteps as he makes his trip to the Cross. I know one fan that was touched by Ernie's witness. Damian Jackson, a former infielder for the Detroit Tigers said, "If I have a few positives I'm going to take out of this year, meeting Ernie [Harwell] is definitely going to be at the top. It was pretty emotional. If he didn't tug at your heart when he was out there talking about the people who meant [so much] to him, his lifetime commitment to his wife, his devotion to God, it was pretty touching. I got a little choked up" (*Ernie Harwell:* Wikipedia, 2010)

Like most of the people profiled in this book, Ernie Harwell accepted Christ Jesus as his Lord and Savior well past his teen years. That demonstrates how personal a relationship with our Lord is.

That relationship cannot be thrust upon a person and be expected to hold. Each of us who choose to follow Him will come to that decision in our own way. Sometimes the decision will be dramatic, and sometimes it will be subtle.

Of all the sports that people can engage in, golf is best known for integrity among the players, especially at the professional level. What other sport relies on the participants to call fouls and penalties on themselves? There have been many instances where golf matches have been lost because a player did something against the rules or signed a scorecard that had inadvertently been filled out incorrectly. Professional golfers hold the rules of their game in high regard.

Anyone over the age of 40, or anyone who is an avid golfer, has heard of the most famous case of golf integrity of the 20th century. The instance was the 1968 Masters Championship at Augusta National Golf Course in Georgia. The golfer was Roberto de Vicenzo. Roberto scored 3 on a par 4 hole, but his playing partner mistakenly recorded a 4 on the card. Roberto missed the error and signed the card as representing his official score. Instead of being tied for the lead at the end of the regulation 72 holes with an opportunity to play another round for the win, Roberto lost the tournament. Being a man of integrity, and knowing the rules that all golfers agree to live by, he took the loss in stride and moved on. That's the story of Roberto de Vicenzo that most people remember. However, it's not the story that defines his true character. That story took place some time later after a tournament in Argentina.

As the story goes, Roberto was leaving a tournament that he had just won when a woman approached him in the parking lot. She said she was a single mother and her child was very sick. She had no insurance and couldn't pay the doctor or hospital for her child's treatment. Roberto immediately endorsed the winner's check to the woman and went on his way. A couple of weeks later a PGA official reported to Roberto that someone had observed his conversation with the woman and decided to investigate. It was determined that the woman was a fraud. There had been no sick child. The rest of the conversation went like this, (Zigler, 2010).

> De Vicenzo asked, "You mean there was no sick baby who is dying?"

"That's right."

De Vicenzo sighed, "That's the best news I've heard all week."

Zigler put Roberto's concern, or lack of it, in perspective with his character by stating,

> How many of you think de Vincenzo really brooded the rest of his life over that woman who had beaten him out of that check? I don't think he gave it another thought. He was truly glad that there had not been an ill child. Now that takes compassion, it takes heart, but it also takes wisdom.
>
> A heart like his, one that is honest, expects the best and holds no malice. It is developed over a lifetime. Roberto de Vincenzo at some point decided he was responsible for his circumstances in life, that he had control over how he responded to disappointment, and that a good attitude and a trusting heart offered many more rewards than their counterparts (Zigler, 2010).

I don't think the 20th century produced a greater leader who demonstrated the attribute of integrity more than President Ronald Reagan (1911 – 2004). President Reagan didn't force his faith upon the American people, but he didn't hide it under a basket either. He actively sought God's guidance and surrounded himself with people of a like passion. Paul told the people of Galatia, "If we live by the Spirit, let us also walk by the Spirit" (Galatians 5:25 ESV). I believe President Reagan endeavored to live those words during his presidency. Peter said, "But just as he who called you is holy, so be holy in all you do…" (1 Peter 1:15 NIV). Based on the humility of the man, I imagine President Reagan would downplay his own holiness and claim to be a sinner just as we are. However, his actions demonstrated that he understood he was called to be an example to others of how we should live the new command that

Jesus handed down through the gospel of John, "A new command I give you: Love one another. As I have loved you, so you must love one another. By this all men will know that you are my disciples, if you love one another" (John 13:34-35 NIV).

At a Dallas Ecumenical Prayer Breakfast, President Reagan stated his position on God's role in our lives as,

> Without God, there is no virtue, because there's no prompting of the conscience. Without God, we're mired in the material, that flat world that tells us only what the senses perceive. Without God, there is a coarsening of the society. And without God, democracy will not and cannot long endure. If we ever forget that we're one nation under God, then we will be a nation gone under.
>
> I-- If I -- If I could just make a personal statement of my own: In these three-and-a-half years I have understood and known better than ever before the words of Lincoln, when he said that he would be the greatest fool on this footstool called Earth if he ever thought that for one moment he could perform the duties of that Office without help from One who is stronger than all (Reagan, 1984).

Ronald Reagan loved and respected everyone and that same love was returned to him. In his farewell speech he recounted this incident that took place on the streets of Moscow.

> But life has a way of reminding you of big things through small incidents. Once, during the heady days of the Moscow summit, Nancy and I decided to break off from the entourage one afternoon to visit the shops on Arbat Street -- that's a little street just off Moscow's main shopping area. Even though our visit was a surprise, every Russian there immediately recognized us and called out our names and reached for our hands. We were just about swept away by the warmth. You could

> almost feel the possibilities in all that joy. But within seconds, a KGB detail pushed their way toward us and began pushing and shoving the people in the crowd. It was an interesting moment. It reminded me that while the man on the street in the Soviet Union yearns for peace, the government is Communist. And those who run it are Communists, and that means we and they view such issues as freedom and human rights very differently (Reagan, 1989).

He believed that the greatest nation on earth has a responsibility to hold other nations accountable for how their citizens are treated and how their freedoms, especially the freedom to worship God, are curtailed. He followed through on those beliefs because he was truly a man of integrity. On June 12, 1987, he called for General Secretary Gorbachev of the Soviet Union to, "tear down this wall!" - the wall that separated East and West Germany. In 1989, after 28 years of separating East and West Germany, the wall came down.

In his first presidential inaugural address, President Reagan addressed the issue of heroes around us. He said, as I am espousing in this book, that the appropriate heroes are among us, we just need to know how to recognize them. He told the American people,

> We have every right to dream heroic dreams. Those who say that we're in a time when there are not heroes, they just don't know where to look. You can see heroes every day going in and out of factory gates. Others, a handful in number, produce enough food to feed all of us and then the world beyond. You meet heroes across a counter, and they're on both sides of that counter. There are entrepreneurs with faith in themselves and faith in an idea who create new jobs, new wealth and opportunity. They're individuals and families whose taxes support the government and whose voluntary gifts support church, charity, culture, art,

and education. Their patriotism is quiet, but deep. Their values sustain our national life.

Now, I have used the words ``they" and ``their" in speaking of these heroes. I could say ``you" and ``your," because I'm addressing the heroes of whom I speak -- you, the citizens of this blessed land. Your dreams, your hopes, your goals are going to be the dreams, the hopes, and the goals of this administration, so help me God (Reagan, 1981).

President Reagan had a philosophy about how to solve all of the problems we face every day. His simple philosophy was, "Within the covers of that single Book are all the answers to all the problems that face us today, if we'd only look there" (Reagan, 1983). As you take time to reflect on this chapter, remember those words.

Time of Reflection

Read 1 Kings 9:4-5; Job 2:3, 9; 6:28-30; 27:2-6; Psalm 25:21; Proverbs 10:9; Titus 2:7-8

- So many passages relate integrity to trusting or fearing God. Why is integrity such an important attribute for a Christian?
- If integrity simply means "doing what you say you are going to do", can you be a person of integrity and not follow God? In other words, if a person tells another person he is going to kill him and does, is the killer a person of integrity? How does God want us to view integrity?
- Job kept hanging on to one thing, his integrity. How easy or difficult was it for Job to maintain his integrity? Could you hang on to your integrity if faced with Job's suffering?
- The proverb of Solomon is pretty explicit regarding integrity. How might a person reveal that they are on a crooked path versus walking securely?
- As Christians we believe in the timelessness of the Word of God. How does Paul's direction for Titus apply to us today?

Courage of Conviction/Covenant

> When Abram was ninety-nine years old,
> he Lord appeared to him and said, "I am God Almighty,
> walk before me and be blameless. I will confirm my covenant
> between me and you and will greatly increase your numbers."
> - Genesis 17:1-2 (NIV)

Courage of conviction is reflected in a person who is determined to stick to a strong, core belief. Similarly, a covenant is the binding agreement between two or more parties. God is determined to honor His covenant with us no matter how many times we lose the courage of our conviction to honor Him.

Early in Lance Sijan's (1942 – 1968) life he learned the meaning of comradeship, fidelity, and patriotism. To him, fidelity, "a faithfulness to something to which someone is bound by pledge or duty" (fidelity, 2010), was as sacred as God's covenant with Abram, and with us. The lessons he learned in his early years would provide him strength as he struggled to evade capture after his plane went down on a bombing mission over the Ho Chi Minh trail in Laos on November 9, 1967. The Military Code of Conduct was another discipline that became a part of who he was. The Code of Conduct is a set of principles and expectations for all military personnel to adhere to in the event of capture and interrogation. For Cpt. Lance Sijan, those principles were his life and his strict adherence to them cost him his life, but his stubborn determination and resistance served as an example and source of strength for other prisoners, among them, Sen. John McCain.

It's hard to appreciate the impact Lance's sacrifice had, and continues to have, on others without knowing the events surrounding his capture, escape, recapture, torture, and death. His story has been told by many different writers. The best story of Lance's life and sacrifice can be found in the book, *Into the Mouth of the Cat* by Malcolm McConnell. The following are excerpts from John McCain's book *Faith of My Fathers.* It is an account that he learned from the two other prisoners, Bob Craner and Guy Gruters, who were with Cpt. Sijan through most of his ordeal. Their actual account is worth viewing at http://www.mishalov.com/Sijan.html.

John McCain writes,

> Air Force Captain Lance Sijan was shot down near Vinh on November 9, 1967. For a day and a half, he lay semiconscious on the ground, grievously injured, with a compound fracture of his left leg, a brain concussion, and a fractured skull. He made radio contact with rescue aircraft, but they were unable to locate him in the dense jungle. On November 11, they abandoned the search.
> Crawling on the jungle floor at night, Lance fell into a sinkhole further injuring himself. For six weeks he evaded capture. On Christmas Day, starved, racked with pain, he passed out on a dirt road, where a few hours later the North Vietnamese found him. Thus began the most inspiring POW story of the war, a story of one man's peerless fidelity to our Code of Conduct. To Lance Sijan, the Code was not an abstract ideal, but the supreme purpose of his life (p. 249-250).
>
> A short time after he was captured, he overpowered an armed guard and managed to escape, taking the guard's rifle with him. Recaptured several hours later, he was tortured as punishment for his escape attempt and for military information. He refused to provide his captors anything beyond what the Code allowed. By the time he reached Hanoi, he was close to death (p. 251).
>
> Interrogated several times, he refused to say anything. He was savagely beaten for his silence, kicked repeatedly and struck with a bamboo club. Bob and Guy heard him scream profanities at his tormentors, and then, after he had endured hours of torture, they heard him say in a weak voice: 'Don't

> you understand? I'm not going to tell you anything. I can't talk to you. It's against the Code.'
>
> Bob and Guy tried to comfort him during his last hours. Working in shifts timed to the tolling of a nearby church bell, they cradled his head in their laps, talked quietly to him of his courage and faith, told him to hang on. Occasionally he shook off his delirium to joke with his cellmates about his circumstances.
>
> Near the end, the guards came for him. Lance knew they were taking him away to die. As they placed him on a stretcher, he said to his friends, 'It's over…it's over.' He called to his father for help as the guards carried him away (p. 251).

Reading his story, I couldn't help but think of Jesus as He was tortured, scorned, ridiculed, and mocked by the Roman guards and led off to die on the Cross. Lance Sijan was carried off by his captors on a litter of wood to die because he wouldn't submit to their demands. As he was carried out his last words were in anguish seeking his father as well. Cpt. Lance Sijan's example lives on today and continues to inspire people to follow in his footsteps. In fact, I found a site that contained the posting from a young AFROTC (Air Force Reserve Officer Training Corp) cadet below. The message speaks for itself (*virtual wall*: Sijan, 2006).

> 14 Nov 2006
> Capt Sijan,
>
> I am a cadet in AFROTC Detachment 895. I am to write a paper about an Air Force leader, and when I discovered the incredible journey you had gone through, I knew that I had to write about it and let other cadets know about the sacrifices you made.
>
> The POC constantly stress the Articles of the Code of Conduct. The first time I read them, I knew the importance of them; however, I never fathomed how one man could endure so much and still have

the discipline to follow them. Whenever I read the Code of Conduct now, I cannot help but think of your story. Because of you, and the countless others who have also given their all for this country, it makes me even prouder to know what I am doing.

You are a true inspiration. You have raised my standards, and I can only hope to internalize the Code as much as you had. I thank God for blessing this earth with people such as yourself. I am proud to serve in the same service as you, and I will strive my hardest to not let you down. I cannot begin to explain how grateful I am to you. Thank you, and you are never going to be forgotten.

Kirk Cameron didn't have a covenant relationship with God; in fact, he had been conditioned to believe in atheism, but God had other plans for the teen heartthrob of the television show *Growing Pains.* God's covenant relationship extends to all of us and He wasn't going to give up on Kirk until he joined the flock.

Kirk was 17 when he began to feel there was something missing in his life. That was hard for him to understand since he had already achieved what some people strive a life-time for and still fall short. Kirk could have had everything he wanted including any young woman he desired. He considered himself to be an intellectual, free-thinking person, so why did he need God? In *Still Growing* he wrote, "But the big questions wouldn't leave me alone. *How did we get here? Does it really matter how I live my life? Does anyone really care? Could there be a God? What will happen to me when I die?"* (p. 129). Kirk didn't realize it at the time, but the Holy Spirit was working all around him through stage hands, friends, and even strangers in Kirk's daily life. He said, "I must have been asking my spiritual questions out loud, because a set designer gave me a book she promised would change my life. It was called *YOU"* (p. 129). The book is really all about "you" the individual and not about you as a part of a larger body with a mission of service, and being a Christ-like example to others. The book didn't answer any of Kirk's burning questions, but it did bring him to a realization that *he* wasn't a god, and certainly not The God, if there was one.

Shortly after that encounter he met a sweet girl on the set and they started dating. She asked him to go to church with her and her family. He wrote,

> To be perfectly honest, I didn't want to go. But I accepted the invitation – not because I was interested in religion, but because I didn't want to offend her family.
>
> It was a big church. The head honcho was a man named Chuck Swindoll. He had a booming voice and spoke with authority. I listened as he read from a Bible, which I thought was nothing more than a book full of rules designed to suck the fun out of life. This pastor began to share the biblical description of God in terms I had never heard before, in a way that grabbed my attention and dazzled my intellect.
>
> He spoke of God's omnipotence: God is *all-powerful.* He talked about God's omniscience: He is *all-knowing.* And he addressed God's holiness. He is *morally perfect* and, therefore, He alone defines what is good (p. 130).

Whether it was the intellectual challenge, or the feeling that the passion that was burning inside of him was finally being satisfied, Kirk was moving in the direction God had planned for him. Kirk began to think,

> *If God is real and eternal, and made everything out of nothing as the Bible says, it makes sense that He also knows every piece of His creation intimately. That means there is nothing He does not know. God knows not only what's at the outer edges of time and space, He also knows who shot JFK, and the details of the secret love lives of the fleas on the back of every cat. That means He also*

knows every thought and every intention of my heart (p. 130-131).

Kirk was not squeaky clean Mr. Green Jeans. His secret thought life and private actions betrayed that image. He realized that he was a sinner, but rather than throwing in the towel and giving up any hope for salvation, Kirk questioned people for more information on God's saving grace. He struggled with turning his life over to Christ for a long time.

Kirk was a science enthusiast. There had to be hard evidence somewhere that would verify the existence of God. He determined to, "Follow the evidence wherever it led, regardless of my own personal bias" (p. 132-133).

As he wrestled with his personal relationship with Christ, he became increasingly aware that some of the things he was doing on and off camera were not in keeping with God's commands. There is a particular incident that Kirk wrote about that indicates how he was turning the corner in building a relationship with Jesus. On one of the shows the script called for his character, Mike, to play a bedroom scene that would later be disclosed as a dream. Kirk confronted the writers and told them, "Dream sequence or not, I didn't like the idea of viewers seeing Mike so casually in bed with a woman." They were surprised by his attitude and questioned him about his motivation. He told them, "I know I have a responsibility as a role model, and parents trust us to be able to watch this show with their kids. I just don't want to do anything that would give kids the idea that I have a casual attitude about sleeping around" (p. 136-138).

Kirk carried that attitude with him from that day forward. His career took a number of different directions, but he never stopped solidifying his relationship with Jesus. Kirk is now an evangelist, a writer, movie director and producer, and actor, besides being a husband and father. When Kirk married Chelsea Noble he made the same vow as every man makes during the wedding ceremony. However, for Kirk, his vow was not just a bunch of touchy, feely, sounds-good words. For him marriage is indeed a covenant relationship. If you have seen the movie *Fireproof* you should be familiar with the final scene where Kirk's character reconciles with his wife. The scene required Kirk to kiss his movie wife, but the scene is actually shot with his real wife, Chelsea. Kirk couldn't think of doing the scene any other way (*Fireproof*, 2008). God told Adam, "For this reason a man will leave his father and mother and be united to his wife, and they will become one flesh" (Gen 2:24 NIV). Kirk honors his covenant relationship with Chelsea just as God honors His covenant with us. God will not forsake us and Kirk will not forsake Chelsea for another.

As Christians, do we have a covenant relationship with our fellow man? Do we have the courage of conviction to do what's right for people who are in situations that overwhelm their ability to break away? I imagine most Christians would agree that we have a responsibility to all mankind and that we should be advocates for the rights of those who are not able to claim their rights for themselves, but few of us step out in faith to honor that covenant. Maybe we adults are too concerned with image, politics, or jeopardizing our own position or status to get involved. Jesus often used children in His stories to demonstrate how we should be trusting and unpretentious in our journey with Him. In Matthew 18:3-4 Jesus tells us, "I tell you the truth, unless you change and become like little children, you will never enter the kingdom of heaven. Therefore, whoever humbles himself like this child is the greatest in the kingdom of heaven."

Children don't carry all the baggage of an adult so they boldly venture into places that we won't, or that we feel are out of our comfort zone. I find it hard to believe that a 12-year-old understands what a covenant relationship is, but my research uncovered over a million children around the world who have developed a covenant relationship with each other on behalf of their peers who can't break away from repression or exploitation that consume their daily life. All of these children belong to an organization called Free the Children, which was founded in 1995 by then 12-year-old Craig Kielburger, his brother Marc, and eleven other children from his 7th grade class. They had never experienced failure before so they had no trepidation launching a campaign to end child labor. Their tenacity and dedication to that objective would eventually spread around the globe reaching children in 45 countries.

Craig was moved to action by a story he read in the paper about a 12-year-old boy in Pakistan who had been murdered for speaking out against child labor. The boy, Iqbal Masih, had been a slave laborer in a carpet factory for six years before he escaped at age ten. Craig felt called by God to do something to end that kind of exploitation. In Luke 10:21 Jesus says, "I praise you, Father, Lord of heaven and earth, because you have hidden these things from the wise and learned, and revealed them to little children. Yes, Father, for this was your good pleasure." Adults had read the same story and were undoubtedly angry, upset, or frustrated, but an appropriate response had been hidden from them. Instead, God revealed the appropriate response to Craig Kielburger.

Craig took the story to his classmates who were as appalled as Craig. They decided that action was necessary and formed Free the Children. At the My Hero Project website, where Craig and Marc hold the honor of being named Peacemaker Heroes, Craig explains the role of Free the Children as,

> While working to change adult attitudes, FTC focuses on empowering youth. 'If you expose young people to the issues of poverty, war, violence and child labor, it's not as if you're taking away their childhood. Young people see it in the world,' says Kielburger. 'We know there are social injustices. FTC is trying to help young people to not just close their eyes and feel [powerless], but to realize that they do have a positive role to play through very simple, very concrete, actions. Maybe it's a petition, or a letter-writing campaign, or a small fundraiser like a bake sale or a car wash. But it empowers them to realize they can make a difference on some level. And it teaches them that even small actions can help change the world. It creates a sense of civic responsibility, a duty, a sense of global citizenship. It's planting that seed' (Jacobs, 2005)

God promises that if we are convicted to Him, He will honor our prayers, provide for our needs, and not give us a Cross too heavy for us to carry. Craig and his 7th grade classmates demonstrated that if we have the courage to act on our conviction we can create, encourage, and participate in change beyond imagination.

Tim Tebow may be putting his professional football career on the line by following his own conviction, but he is willing to take the risk because the reward is greater than the consequences. Tim, Florida Gators quarterback and one of the top NFL draft candidates for 2010, is taking a pro-life stand that will put him and his mother, Pam, center stage at the 2010 Super Bowl. A number of sports experts are saying his prospects may be narrowed and that he could lose money in a potentially lucrative contract deal if some of the team agents drop him as a choice. Tim's response was, "...then it probably wouldn't be a good fit for me in the first place, because I'm never going to deny what I believe in" (Volin, 2010).

Tim, the son of missionary parents Bob and Pam Tebow, was born in Manila in the Philippines. His mother contracted a life-threatening illness during pregnancy. The medications used to bring her out of a coma and treat her dysentery attributed to a severe placental abruption, a significant contributor to maternal mortality. Pam's doctors recommended she have an abortion to protect her life, which she refused. She trusted in the Lord instead of the advice of her doctors and the Lord protected her and her baby. Experiencing God's healing grace in such a profound way convicted Pam and Tim that abortion is not a legitimate option for a difficult or unwanted pregnancy. Tim is putting face and value on the 1,000,000+ abortions that occur annually.

There is a growing number of people who consider Tim Tebow to be the most gifted and talented young athlete of all time. Tim is honored by all of the accolades that he has received, but he gives all of the glory to God and is not shy about his convictions. Upon reading the palmbeachpost.com article, one woman posted the following comment:

> What an inspiration and show of character! I am so tired of hearing from humans who received the gift of life [and] are so threatened by someone who was born from a mother that was willing to chance her own life to give her son life. They are truly children of God, I admire this young man. Shame

> on anyone that belittles him for showing gratitude for "His own Right to Life!" In the end those that oppose life will have someone higher to answer to. (A pro-life Mother!, 2010)

Another woman posted a note at the Huffington Post Website that captures the reason for this book in a few short sentences. She wrote:

> It saddens me to know that there are still so many people who don't know what they're here for - to glorify God. The talent that God has placed in Tim on the football field is extraordinary, but the gift of spreading His word is so much more than that. Those "little verses" [Tim's eye black Bible passages] touch more lives than you may realize. My four old wants to be just like Tebow! Not only because he's a phenomenal football player, but because he loves Jesus Christ. Tim is an amazing minister. Through those verses he spreads God's word without saying anything, and millions of people see it every Sat.

As I mentioned at the opening of this chapter, courage of conviction is reflected in a person's determination to stick to a strong, core belief. Hermine (Miep) Gies (1909 – 2010) is an example of that kind of conviction. In fact, she and her husband, Jan, and four of their friends put their lives on the line as a measure of the seriousness of their conviction. If you aren't familiar with Jan and Miep Gies, you may be familiar with the family they protected during World War II – the Frank family including Anne and four other Jews.

Miep worked for Otto Frank, a spice business owner in Holland. When Nazis started rounding up Dutch Jews for deportation to concentration camps in July 1942, Otto asked Miep and her friends to hide his family in an annex of his spice warehouse. Miep's response was, "I answered, 'Yes, of course.' It seemed perfectly natural to me. I could help these people. They were powerless, they didn't know where to turn" (Associated Press, 2010). For 25 months,

Miep, Jan, and Miep's friends fed and clothed the Frank family at great risk of their own lives. Even after the Franks were discovered and taken as prisoners, Miep continued to ignore her own welfare by going to the police station to offer a bribe for their release. However, the measure was in vain since the Franks had already been shipped to a concentration camp.

Miep and the others were honored for their courage of conviction, but Miep resisted becoming a character study of heroism for young people. In a 1997 online chat with schoolchildren she said, "I don't want to be considered a hero…Imagine young people would grow up with the feeling that you have to be a hero to do your human duty. I am afraid nobody would ever help other people, because who is a hero? I was not. I was just an ordinary housewife and secretary" (Associated Press, 2010). Hopefully young and old alike will recognize her not for her good works, but for her motivation to be Christ to people who were not in a position to speak for themselves or to live as they would allow others to live. To honor her request to remain out of the spotlight, I will simply refer to her as an invisible hero.

Conor Oberst said something that fits the relationship between the Gies and the Franks well. He said, "I came upon a doctor who appeared in quite poor health. I said, 'There's nothing that I can do for you that you can't do for yourself.' He said, 'Oh yes you can. Just hold my hand. I think that that would help.' So I sat with him a while then I asked him how he felt. He said, 'I think I'm cured'" (Conor Oberst, n. d.). The Franks weren't cured, but the conviction that Jan, Miep, and the other spice factory workers displayed was of great comfort in a horribly difficult time.

Time of Reflection

Read Jeremiah 31:31-34; Luke 22:20-22; 1 Corinthians 11:23-28

- Jeremiah makes many references to the covenant relationship between God and the Israelites. God continued to honor his covenant with them, but they continued to shun their responsibility in that covenant relationship. How do you think we are doing as a church and as a nation in our covenant relationship with God?
- It takes great courage for a person to stand up for his or her convictions. How do you think we might fare as a nation if

we were challenged to stand for our convictions? Would it be easier to stand firm as a Body of Christ than as an individual Christian? Discuss what that means concerning the strength of our convictions.
- Jesus said, "This cup is the new covenant in my blood..." Have we been offered the final covenant from God? What happens if we break the covenant this time?
- God brought judgment on the entire nation of Israel even though there were some who were living by the Law. Does the new covenant through the blood of Jesus apply to each person alone or are we accountable as a nation as well?

Compassion/Mercy

> "Compassion is not just an emotion; it is an action demonstrating a sincere effort to relieve the suffering of another"
> -Unknown

The concordance of my NIV Bible has ninety references to God's compassion for His people. Regardless of how many times we have fallen short of honoring our covenant with Him, He has never forsaken us. He has punished us for our sins and unbelief, but He has always shown compassion and taken us back into His fold. Jeremiah told the people of Judah and Jerusalem:

> This is what the Lord says: "As for all my wicked neighbors who seize the inheritance I gave my people Israel, I will uproot them from their lands and I will uproot the house of Judah from among them. But after I uproot them, I will again have compassion and will bring each of them back to his own inheritance and his own country" (Jeremiah 12:14-15 NIV).

Paul also addressed compassion in his letter to the people of Colosse. In emphasizing the rules for a godly life he wrote, "Therefore, as God's chosen people holy and dearly loved, clothe yourselves with compassion, kindness, humility, gentleness and patience. Bear with each other and forgive whatever grievances you may have against one another. Forgive as the Lord forgave you. And over all these virtues put on love, which binds them all together in perfect unity" (Colossians 3:12-14 NIV).

Compassion is often viewed as a person's desire to relieve the distress of others. Jesus gives us an example of that in Mark when He healed a man with leprosy. Mark wrote, "A man with leprosy came to him and begged him on his knees, 'if you are willing, you can make me clean.' Filled with compassion, Jesus reached out his hand and touched the man, 'I am willing,' he said. 'Be clean!' Immediately the leprosy left him and he was cured" (Mark 1:40-42 NIV). There are many people, including clergy, who believe that only Christ Jesus had the power of healing. Paul tells us in 1 Corinthians 12 that we all have gifts. Some have even been given the gift of healing by the Holy Spirit. What a wonderful gift for showing compassion to others.

I haven't attended a medical training class of any kind, but the compassion I see demonstrated by EMT personnel, nurses, doctors, and other medial professionals leads me to believe that compassion is a subject that gets much attention in the classroom. I haven't met a medical professional that doesn't seem to be teeming with compassion. It isn't possible to profile all of the compassionate caregivers in the space provided in this book so I have to wrap them up in the couple of examples that follow.

Although compassion is a Christ-like attribute, showing compassion doesn't make a person like Christ if that person is not living his or her life for Him. A number of compassionate medical professionals have come into my life, but I've never had one pray with me or for me for the healing blood of Jesus to be upon me or my family member. Dr. Ben Carson is the exception to that observation. I don't personally know Dr. Carson, but I know of him, and I think others need to know of him as well.

Dr. Carson's childhood environment would not be characterized as atypical for an aspiring medical professional, especially for a man who would become one of the world's most renowned neurosurgeons. He was blessed with a loving mother who instilled in him the motivation to rise above his environment. His mother insisted that he and his brother read two books a week and then submit a report to her for each book. They also couldn't watch more than three television shows a week, but they could select their own shows. Ben loved Saturday morning science programs and developed a passion for learning all he could about the world around him. His mother did domestic work so there was little money for extravagancies such as stylish clothes. That bothered Ben, but, like many other lessons he learned growing up, his mother used that to teach him about what really counts in life. In his book, *Gifted Hands – The Ben Carson Story,* he notes one such occasion. His mother told him, "Bennie, what's inside counts the most. Anybody can dress up on the outside and be dead on the inside" (p. 46). Although his mother never completed grade school, she was a wonderful teacher of the lessons of both a secular and Christian life.

Dr. Carson's gift of compassion didn't come easy for him. He had a terrible temper, which is not a good foundation for compassion. He recounts one instance in the ninth grade when he lost control and tried to kill one of his friends with a knife. He recognized that Satan was controlling his actions through his quick temper and searched for an answer. He recalled how his mother taught him to lift up his concerns to the Lord and how his Christian school teachers had told him and his classmates that God would help them if they only asked Him. Young Ben knew his only solution was to lay his anger at the foot of the Cross and pray for God to help him. He prayed, "Lord," I whispered, "You have to take this temper from me. If You don't, I'll never be free from it. I'll end up doing things a lot worse than trying to stab one of my best friends" (p. 59). To demonstrate the miracle that took place in that moment he continues,

> Already heavy into psychology (I had been reading *Psychology Today* for a year), I knew that temper was a personality trait. Standard thinking in the field pointed out the difficulty, if not the impossibility, of modifying personality traits. Even today some experts believe that the best we can do is accept our limitations and adjust to them.
> Tears streamed between my fingers. 'Lord, despite what all the experts tell me, You can change me. You can free me forever from this destructive personality trait.'
> I wiped my nose on a piece of toilet paper and let it drop on the floor. 'You've promised that if we come to You and ask something in faith, that You'll do it. I believe that You can change this in me' (p. 59).
>
> At one point I'd slipped out of the bathroom long enough to grab a Bible. Now I opened it and began to read in Proverbs. Immediately I saw a

> string of verses about angry people and how they get themselves into trouble. Proverbs 16:32 impressed me the most: 'He who is slow to anger is better than the mighty, and he who rules his spirit than he who takes a city' (RSV).
> My lips moved wordlessly as I continued to read. I felt as though the verses had been written just to me, for me. The words of Proverbs condemned me, but they also gave me hope. After a while peace began to fill my mind. My hands stopped shaking. My tears stopped. During those hours alone in the bathroom, something happened to me. God heard my deep cries of anguish. A feeling of lightness flowed over me, and I knew a change of heart had taken place. I felt different. I was different (p. 60).
>
> I'm not afraid of anything as long as I think of Jesus Christ and my relationship to Him and remember that the One who created the universe can do anything. I also have evidence – my own experience – that God can do anything, because He changed me (p.61).

Those of us who have experienced such a blessing can empathize with Dr. Carson's account. God will indeed respond to our prayers for His intervention in our lives. He assures us of that in Matthew 7:7-8 where Jesus said, "Ask and it will be given to you; seek and you will find; knock and the door will be opened to you. For everyone who asks receives; he who seeks finds; and to him who knocks, the door will be opened" (NIV).

As a result of his mother's inspiration and his own passion for learning, Ben improved from a less than marginal student to the top of his class in school. He easily met the requirements for medical school, but attaining passing grades in college required far more focus than Ben had needed in high school. He recounts another time when he had to call on the Lord to help him through a difficult situation. He needed to do well on a final exam at Yale, but didn't have the time or capacity to learn the required material. Tired from cramming for the exam, he went before the Lord,

> 'God, I'm sorry. Please forgive me for failing You and for failing myself.' Then I slept. While I slept I had a strange dream, and, when I awakened in the morning, it remained as vivid as if it had actually happened. In the dream I was sitting in the chemistry lecture hall, the only person there. The door opened, and a nebulous figure walked in the room, stopped at the board, and started working out chemistry problems. I took notes of everything he wrote (p. 79).

As Ben opened his test booklet the next morning he was amazed to find that the problems were exactly the same as those from his dream. Actually, he shouldn't have been amazed at all. After all, he had taken his petition before the Lord and should have been confident that He would respond in a most profound way.

Dr. Carson tells of a particularly difficult case involving an 11-month-old girl. In *Gifted Hands* he refers to her as Jennifer. He operated on Jennifer twice resulting in the complete removal of the right hemisphere of her brain. Although the operations went well, Jennifer arrested. Dr. Carson recalls praying, "God, please, please don't let her die. Please" (p. 165). Jennifer didn't respond to the lifesaving efforts of the staff. God answered Ben's prayer, but, as sometimes happens, the response was no. Dr. Carson learned that compassion takes on many forms. In Jennifer's case he had compassion for her condition and used all of his skill to provide a quality life for her, and within hours he was *sharing* compassion with her parents as they all grieved her loss.

Dr. Carson believes his skill as a surgeon is truly a gift of God. He tells patients that he is just an instrument that God uses for His will. Ben prays with patients, encourages the patient's family to pray for comfort, strength, and healing. He also prays while he prepares for surgery and during surgery. In one particularly difficult case he recalls,

> Every time I touched the stem, it bled. My assistant continued to suction up the blood to keep the site clear while I asked myself, *What do I do now?* I prayed silently and fervently, *God, help me know what to do.*
>
> I always pray before any of the operations, as I scrub, standing at the table before I begin. This time I was actually conscious of praying during the entire surgery as I kept thinking, *Lord, it's up to You. You've got to do something here.* I had no idea what to try.
>
> I paused and stared into space as I said to God, *Craig will die unless You show me what to do.* Within seconds, I knew – a kink of intuitive knowledge filled my mind. 'Let me have the laser,' I said to the technician (p. 198-199).

Dr. Carson dedicates his life to relieving the stress of others. He has found that prayer not only relieves the stress of those who need his care, but it relieves his stress as well so he can respond as God guides him.

Another doctor who believes in the healing powers of prayer is Dale A. Matthews, M.D. Dr. Matthews, author of *The Faith Factor – is Religion Good for Your Health,* believes that faith and medicine go hand-in-hand. In a July 1999 *Guidepost* article he said, "The words of the Bible can have a healing effect on my patients' physical and emotional recovery" (p. 32). He didn't always believe that though. He was taken by surprise when a patient asked him to pray with him. Dr. Matthews responded with a quick prayer and went on with his business of applying scientific practice to the man's condition. He admits the prayer had calming effects on the patient and began to wonder how large a role faith played in the healing process. As more people requested him to pray with or for them, he "started to look to the Bible, along with my Physician's Desk Reference and prescription pad, as tools of my trade" (p. 32). The article continues,

When the Bible says "Direct me in the path of your commands, for there I find delight" (Psalm 119:35), it seems to be literally *true* – and delight certainly offers a positive state receptive to healing. Steady doses of "Be strong, and of good courage. Fear not..." (1 Chronicles 22:13) can be beneficial for someone facing surgery.

"Let not your heart be troubled..." (John 14:1) may do wonders for someone worrying about the toll of chronic incapacitation or developing illness. After all, "Pleasant words are as a honeycomb, sweet to the soul, and health to the bones" (Proverbs 16:24).

Another reason the Bible helps people get better is because it enables them to reframe their problems in a more constructive way.

Whether about warding off depression ("The cheerful heart has a continual feast"; Proverbs 15:15) or getting the necessary rest ("Remember the Sabbath...you shall not do any work..."; Exodus 20:8, 10), the Bible is full of sound advice.

As a physician, I believe we can effectively aid our healing by turning to God with a willing heart. That's why among the latest medical books lining my office, there will always be a place for the Holy Bible, the great handbook of healing (p. 32 – 33).

There is an EMT from our church who also finds prayer gives him comfort and strength as he assists people in need. His name is Jamie Balcom and he is not only an EMT, but he is a seminary student and youth pastor. Jamie said the first thing he does while preparing to aid the patient is pray. He prays for healing for the person, comfort and strength for the family, and calmness and guidance for him and his partners. As you can imagine his life is overflowing with responsibility, but with Jesus leading the way, there are no barriers too strong or no obstacles too difficult for him to overcome. Just as Jamie has compassion on those that he serves in ministry and in life-threatening situations, so Christ Jesus has compassion on him so he can meet the challenges of the ever changing world of an EMT professional.

God uses many different venues to teach us the gift of compassion. Sometimes the lessons require a slap in the face or a kick in the butt to get our attention. Millard Fuller received one of those attention-getters in his lesson on compassion.

Being a millionaire by age 29 is a lofty goal that requires a lot of dedication, time, persistence, perseverance, and setting aside of other priorities. Striving to achieve that level of success is commendable if the glory and honor are attributed to the Lord and not to human endeavor. If the Lord is not a part of the formula for achieving success, disaster can become the ultimate result of the wealth attained. Millard Fuller learned that lesson, and he also learned that Christ has compassion on those who turn from their focus on *self* and turn their lives over to Him.

Millard Fuller (1935 – 2009) became a self-made millionaire before he turned 29. He had everything a person could possibly want, except a happy marriage, his health, his integrity, and most of all, a relationship with Christ Jesus. In a materialistic sense he had acquired it all, but lost everything that was important along the way. Fortunately Millard was married to a wonderful woman, Linda, who was committed to the covenant of marriage as God intended and patiently worked with Millard to recognize the destruction that was taking place around him. Subsequent soul-searching by Millard led to reconciliation with Linda, and the renewal of his commitment to Christ.

Following the recommitment of his life to Christ, Millard and Linda did the unthinkable – they sold all of their possessions, gave the money to the poor, and embarked on a journey to discover God's plan for them. The journey led them to Koinonia Farm in Georgia where they teamed with the founder, Clarence Jordan, in a ministry to provide homes for people with low incomes. It was also at Koinonia that Millard and Linda experienced the kind of love and compassion that Paul wrote about in his letter to the church at Philippi. Paul wrote, "If you have any encouragement from being united with Christ, if any comfort from his love, if any fellowship with the Spirit, if any tenderness and compassion, then make my joy complete by being like-minded, having the same love, being one in spirit and purpose. Do nothing out of selfish ambition or vain conceit, but in humility consider others better than yourselves. Each of you should look not only to your own interests, but also to the interests of others" (Philippians 2:1-4 NIV). From that early relationship at Koinonia, and the love and encouragement the Fullers experienced there, emerged God's plan. They believed His plan for them was the world-wide home building ministry we now know as Habitat for Humanity.

Regarding their ministry, Millard said, "I see life as both a gift and a responsibility. My responsibility is to use what God has given me to help people in need" (Millard Fuller – Habitat for Humanity International Founder, 2010). Upon his death, a tribute in *The New York Times* stated, "Mr. Fuller said his inspiration came from the Bible, starting with the injunction in Exodus 22:25 against charging interest to the poor. He spoke of the 'economics of Jesus' and insisted that providing shelter to all was 'a matter of conscience.' *Christianity Today* in 1999 called him 'God's contractor'" (Martin, 2009, February 3). He and Linda were contractors building dwellings for needy families while helping those families build a new life together as children of God.

Linda continues their ministry and is encouraging women to get more involved in home construction projects. One of those outreaches is Women Building A Legacy, in which Linda challenges women to make a positive impact on the future by providing safe, healthy housing where children can flourish and grow. The outreach, spearheaded by women celebrities and U.S. first ladies, has been responsible for the completion of nearly 100 simple, decent, affordable houses built for families in need.

Linda says the Habitat for Humanity ministry reaches the poor as well as those who God has blessed with more financial resources than necessary to support their own needs.

> What the poor need is not charity but capital, not caseworkers but co-workers. And what the rich need is a wise, honorable and just way of divesting

themselves of their overabundance. The Fund for Humanity will meet both of these needs. Money for the fund will come from shared gifts by those who feel they have more than they need and from non-interest bearing loans from those who cannot afford to make a gift but who do want to provide working capital for the disinherited . . . The fund will give away no money. It is not a handout (Linda Fuller – co-founder of Habitat for Humanity International, 2010).

The people profiled above are in positions that allow them to show compassion to many. Some of us don't have that exposure to a large and diverse audience, but that doesn't mean we cannot share the gift of compassion with others. In an earlier chapter I shared how my daughter Lori recently completed the adoption of a 15-year-old Russian orphan. That is an example of compassion for one of God's children just as much as treating thousands of patients or providing homes for hundreds of families. There is another example of individual compassion that I want to share with you. This story is about the compassion of the family of Sean and Leigh Anne Tuohy.

Sean and Leigh Anne were living the good life. They had nice cars, a nice home, and sent their daughter to a fine school. It would have been easy for them to get wrapped up in their own world and not pay any attention to the plight of the truly needy people in their community. But the Tuohys weren't a typical self-absorbed, well-to-do family. In case you aren't familiar with their story, the Tuohys are white, but their son, Michael Oher – right tackle for the Baltimore Ravens - is black. That's the small, inconsequential part of their story though.

The whole story is about the extended Tuohy family, including Michael, and the mutual compassion that blended their diverse backgrounds into a loving, caring body completely dedicated to one another with Christ Jesus at the center of their relationship.

In a *Guidepost* interview of November 9, 2009, Leigh Anne tells how the family's initial response to provide for Michael's needs for shelter, food, and clothing, quickly evolved into meeting his needs for a family he never had. The article states that, "Leigh Anne believes that Michael became a part of the Tuohy family because they stayed open to the opportunities God put before them. 'God had plans for Michael's life, and we just happened to be facilitators of that plan,' she explains. 'We like to think of ourselves as merely the vessels He used to accomplish His purpose in Michael's life'" (Rue, 2009). The article continues,

> Sometimes little opportunities to do good grow beyond our wildest dreams. That's what happened with Michael and the Tuohys. Leigh Anne had no idea at the time that they would eventually adopt Michael. "It didn't really start out as a mission to adopt a homeless kid," says Leigh Anne. "It was more that one thing led to another. When we got to know Michael, it was just sort of 'survival mode' at first as we tried to meet his needs. He needed a place to stay; then we realized he needed to go to the doctor for his vaccinations. Then it was, 'Hey, this kid's never been to the dentist—we'd better get him in to see one.' So it was a matter of firing on all cylinders at once, trying to catch up on 14 years of his life."

The article concludes,
> Leigh Anne says she has a lot of favorite Bible verses, but topping the list is Luke 12:48: "To whom much is given, much is required."
> She explains, "Our story has gone so far so quickly that I definitely believe God's hand is guiding it. I certainly don't think it's a coincidence that the movie [Blind Side] happens to open on National Adoption Day (November 20). God is in charge of this entire project, and we've held on to that."
> Leigh Anne's passion, clearly, is to help homeless children. "Our family has come to understand how many homeless children need to be adopted. I heard a statistic recently that if every church in America would see to it that just one child is

> adopted, the problem of homeless children would disappear. There are thousands of Michaels out there. They may not all be the next great professional football player, but they may be the person who grows up to cure cancer, or becomes a great husband or wife to someone."
>
> For the Tuohys, Michael's story is inspiring not because he became a professional athlete, but because it shows that we can all change people's lives by investing time in individuals (Rue, 2009).

Maybe Michael will be able to respond in-kind to someone in need and become an invisible hero himself.

There's another Mike that I would like to introduce to you who is also surrounded by invisible heroes. This Mike had a reputation of being a problem child that others preferred to ignore rather than show compassion for. Beth Anthony couldn't do that.

Beth's first encounter with Mike was in a Charleston, South Carolina, school cafeteria. In the July 1999 feature *Guidepost* article, "A Place for Mike", Beth describes how Mike was throwing a tantrum and all the other teachers were simply ignoring him because no one seemed to know what to do with him, so they just ignored him until he decided to stop. Beth decided to reach out in an unusual, but loving and compassionate way. She asked Mike to help her find her car because she was afraid of new places. Surprised by her request, Mike crawled out from under a table, took her hand, and led her to the parking lot. Something in his smile and the way he held her hand caused Beth to recognize that Mike had needs that weren't being met, but at that point she felt inadequate to meet those needs. It wasn't long before Mike's needs became so critical that Beth had to enlist the support of her family, and God, to meet them.

A fire destroyed the home that Mike was living in with his aunt and her six children. His aunt could find space for herself and her own family, but someone else would have to take care of Mike until other arrangements could be made. That someone would be Beth, and other arrangements would never develop.

Complicating the situation for the Anthony family, and for Mike, was the fact that Mike is black and the Anthonys are white. In an effort to allow Mike to develop relationships with other black children, Beth enrolled him in a day camp. That turned out to be an embarrassing and troubling situation for Mike, but it provided the forum for a long overdue awakening. Mike had been questioned by his peers about the white woman who was picking him up from camp. He told them that his mother was working and Beth was his baby-sitter. Beth felt the truth needed to be shared so she requested an opportunity to address Mike's class. The *Guidepost* article details that session.

> The following afternoon I sat with Mike at my side before a curious audience, feeling more nervous than I had on my very first day in front of a class. "Once when Mike was learning to ride a bike, he fell down and skinned his knee," I began. "I was cleaning the scrape when he said, 'Look, our blood is the same color!' The color of our skin might be different, but underneath, we're alike.
> "I think God brought Mike into our family to show us that what's on the outside isn't important as long as we love each other on the inside." It was becoming clearer to me as I explained it. "I love Mike and he loves me. That's what makes him my son. That's what really matters."
> Suddenly, there in front of all the kids in the day camp, Mike reached out and grabbed my hand. Like the first time we'd connected back in the school cafeteria, I felt that unforgettable warmth flowing between us.
> Only now I understood it came from God. From the very beginning, he'd been drawing us beyond neglect and prejudice, beyond my doubts and worries, drawing us together with love. And that, in the end, was what Mike, like all of us, needed most (p. 30).

What a wonderful feeling it is to help someone, especially an orphan, or a child without a loving and caring family, or one who is literally all alone in the world. I had an opportunity to be part of an orphan's life while serving in Vietnam. Many years have passed since then, but I think about that privilege often and wonder how that young girl's life turned out. I got to come home after a year "in country." I hope she got a home to go to also.

Samuel Adams (1722 – 1803) expressed God's expectation of us when he addressed the Massachusetts legislature on January 30, 1797, regarding the moral platform that should be put in place to ensure that every American be instilled with the value of love and compassion for one another. He said,

> As Piety, Religion and Morality have a happy influence on the minds of men, in their public as well as private transactions, you will not think it unseasonable, although I have frequently done it, to bring to your remembrance the great importance of encouraging our University, town schools, and other seminaries of education, that our children and youth while they are engaged in the pursuit of useful science, may have their minds impressed with a strong sense of the duties they owe to their God, their instructors and each other, so that when they arrive to a state of manhood, and take a part in any public transactions, their hearts having been deeply impressed in the course of their education with the moral feelings - such feelings may continue and have their due weight through the whole of their future lives (Samuel Adams Quotes, 2010.

There are invisible heroes among us who have been impressed in the course of their lives with the moral feelings. They are all around us. We just need to know what to look for. I hope this glimpse into what the "moral feeling" is will help you discover an invisible hero to emulate.

Time of Reflection

Read Colossians 3:12-14; 1 Corinthians 12:7-11; and Mark 9:36-37 and respond to the following talking points.

- Paul's directive in Colossians is to "God's chosen people..." Discuss how we should be showing compassion to those around us.
- Do we have greater compassion on Christians? If so, discuss how God differentiates between believers and nonbelievers.
- The power of healing is a controversial subject today. Do you believe there are people with the gift of healing, or is healing entirely based on the application of proven medical science? Has your doctor ever prayed with you? Have you asked him or her to do so? Share illustrations of physical healing through the Holy Spirit.
- It has been reported that there wouldn't be any orphans in the United States if every church would arrange a single adoption through one of their church families. Why is it so hard for us to open our homes to children who don't have one of their own?

Repentant

> "Let everyone turn from his evil way
> and from the violent way that is in his hands."
> - Jonah 3:8b (ESV)

When I told my wife, Pat, about the inclusion of this chapter she remarked that repentant was not a Christ-like attribute because Christ Jesus had nothing to be repentant about. Since He lived a sinless life she felt I should exclude repentance and focus on another attribute. Although I agreed with her logic, I reasoned that even though Jesus had nothing to repent for, we do. Isaiah called the nation of Israel to repentance by telling them, "This is what the Sovereign Lord, the Holy One of Israel, says: 'In repentance and rest is your salvation, in quietness and trust is your strength...'" (Isaiah 30:15 NIV). Simon Peter said, "The Lord is not slow in keeping his promise, as some understand slowness. He is patient with you, not wanting anyone to perish, but everyone to come to repentance" (2 Peter 3:9 NIV).

A common Psalm of repentance is Psalm 51. It is David's humble prayer for forgiveness. David prayed:

> Have mercy on me, O God, according to your unfailing love; according to your great compassion blot out my transgressions. Wash away all my iniquity and cleanse me from my sin. For I know my transgressions, and my sin is always before me. Against you, you only, have I sinned and done what is evil in your sight, so that you are proved right when you speak and justified when you judge. Surely I was sinful at birth, sinful from the time my mother conceived me. Surely you desire truth in the inner parts; you teach me wisdom in the inmost place. Cleanse me with hyssop and I will be clean; wash me, and I will be whiter than snow. Let me hear joy and gladness; let the bones you have crushed rejoice. Hide your face from my sins and blot out all my iniquity.

>Create in me a pure heart, O God, and renew a steadfast spirit within me. Do not cast me from your presence or take your Holy Spirit from me. Restore to me the joy of your salvation and grant me a willing spirit to sustain me. Then I will teach transgressors your ways, and sinners will turn back to you. Save me from bloodguilt, O God, the God who saves me, and my tongue will sing of your righteousness. O Lord, open my lips, and my mouth will declare your praise. You do not delight in sacrifice, or I would bring it; you do not take pleasure in burnt offerings. The sacrifices of God are a broken spirit; a broken and contrite heart, O God, you will not despise. In your good pleasure make Zion prosper; build up the walls of Jerusalem. Then there will be righteous sacrifices, whole burnt offerings to delight you; then bulls will be offered on your altar.

"The word reached the king of Nineveh and he arose from his throne, removed his robe, covered himself with sackcloth, and sat in ashes. And he issued a proclamation and published through Nineveh, 'By the decree of the king and his nobles: Let neither man nor beast, herd nor flock, taste anything. Let them not feed or drink water, but let man and beast be covered with sackcloth, and let them call out mightily to God. Let everyone turn from his evil way and from the violent way that is in his hands. Who knows? God may relent and turn from his fierce anger, so that we may not perish.

"When God saw what they did, how they turned from their evil way, God relented of the disaster that he said he would do to them, and he did not do it" (Jonah 3:6-10 ESV).

I don't believe a person or group of people can repent with David's sincerity through a national decree or edict by a ruler. That's probably why the Israelites kept falling out of favor with God. They relied on intercessors to approach God on their behalf instead of seeking Him on their own. God knows our hearts and wants us to come to Him individually as David did in humility and with a contrite heart. Pat Boone shared that same conviction. In his autobiography, *A New Song* (Boone, 1970), Pat tells about the journey he and his family made before they finally surrendered to God's will.

Early in his life, Pat Boone had considered becoming a minister. In fact, he had taken a preaching assignment in a country church in Texas shortly after he and Shirley were married. He was still in college, but felt he was following God's will. He had many opportunities to develop a strong, personal relationship with God during those years in the pulpit. He understood that God has the answer for even the most impossible situations, if he would be still and listen for His guidance.

He could feel God's presence in the early years of his singing career. It seemed every recording went to the "Top Ten" and his popularity opened doors for him in television. His first ethical question came when he was offered his own television show. It would be sponsored by a cigarette manufacturer. Pat struggled with how God expected a Christian to respond to something that was contrary to church doctrine. Although his agents argued that it was the sponsor who was selling the cigarettes and not him, Pat turned down the opportunity. Pat was pleased that he had the strength to make the right moral decision, but his motivation wasn't necessarily God-honoring. Pat's real goal was to be a teacher, so turning down the television program wasn't a career-wrecking decision from that perspective.

When his entertainment career took off he was caught in a dilemma of how to determine, and then, honor God's will. He thought he could be a good Christian in the entertainment industry, and he knew the industry needed Christian leadership, but he soon found out that, although he was well-versed in doctrine, his relationship with Jesus was still weak.

The more successful he became in the entertainment industry, the more he lost sight of a teaching career, and the more distant his relationship with God became. To promote himself and keep his name in front of Hollywood moguls required Pat to develop a social life. His new life involved late-night parties where he was exposed to drinking, smoking, and the temptation of women willing to compromise moral character for his attention. He tried unsuccessfully to balance the new life with the Christian image he wanted the public to see. The more he separated himself from God, the more his career and marriage suffered. In Shirley's attempt to hold their family together, she eventually caved in to the pressure and joined Pat in the party scene. Instead of bringing them closer together the change created a larger void in their relationship. The void could only be filled by God.

Fortunately there were a number of Christians that came alongside Pat and Shirley to help them in their journey back to Jesus Christ. The first was Clint Davidson who witnessed to Pat regarding real miracles that had been a direct response to prayer. Clint told Pat that his wife, Flora, had been in an accident that initiated serious deterioration of her hip. Doctors said the only procedure that would provide some stability was fusing the hip into a rigid position. Flora and Clint prayed for healing and then they attended a group prayer meeting for healing. Upon return from the healing sessions Flora's hip began to heal, the pain ceased, and deterioration not only stopped, but the tissue began a process of rebuilding. Pat wasn't skeptical of the miracle, after all he believed the apostle Paul in his letter to the church in Corinth which states, "To one there is given through the Spirit the message of wisdom, to another the message of knowledge by means of the same Spirit, to another faith by the same Spirit, to another the gifts of healing by that one Spirit, to another miraculous powers, to another prophecy, to another distinguishing between spirits, to another speaking in different kinds of tongues, and to another the interpretation of tongues" (I Cor. 12: 8-10 NIV). However, Pat was raised to believe that those gifts ceased at the end of the fist century. Pat wanted badly to believe that such miracles could occur because both his marriage and his career needed one badly.

Another Christian to come alongside Pat and Shirley was David Wilkerson, author of *The Cross and the Switchblade.* David, who was profiled in an earlier chapter, recounted to Pat a number of miracles that the Holy Spirit had worked among young people of New York City who were trapped by narcotics and a violent life. Pat was so inspired by the work that David was doing that he organized a group of investors to turn David's book into a movie and played the role of David Wilkerson himself, but that's another story. You can rent the movie and see for your self how it comes out. The movie had to sit on the back burner for a while though because Pat was still on his journey back to the Lord and wasn't ready to deliver the passion needed to truly reflect David Wilkerson's commitment to his mission.

The third person to come along side Pat was George Otis. In *A New Song* Pat writes,

> He [Otis] related how once he had no place for God in his life. Then how he became a nominal or middleground Christian, like I was then. Finally, how when he made a *total surrender* as the result of calamities and frustrations, *his whole life changed.* His relationship with God, his family and friends became supercharged with power; his business career flourished. Now God was his partner, 'a Partner who knows tomorrow.

Pat needed that same kind of relationship with his Lord and Savior, and that's what he received as soon as he surrendered his life to Christ again and allowed the Holy Spirit to work in him. He had been going through the motions of being a Christian rather than celebrating the emotions of having the Holy Spirit dwelling within him.

It happened while he was on his way from church to an important meeting one Sunday. He relates how he was praying out loud on the way and it was the first time he every really had a conversation with God. Pat said, "Father, I've really drifted away, haven't I? Is there a way back? I've made an awful lot of mistakes, I know – but I do want to serve you again. I'm sorry for all the things I've done and said, sorry that I've practically frittered away the inheritance you've given me. I pray that you'll bless this show today…and if you do…that you'll use it and me in your will, and most of all that you'll draw me closer to you. I need you, Father…I need you…" He says his prayer might have been a bit selfish, but he was honestly repentant and wanted the Holy Spirit to work in him and through him. Pat Boone hasn't deviated from his journey since that time of confession.

It's one thing to know Jesus, drift away, feel lost, repent, and return to Him, but it is quite another thing to set out to discredit the Word of God and in the process develop a deep, abiding love for Christ. That's what happened to Lee Strobel.

In *The Case for Christ* Lee takes the reader on a journey through his investigation to discredit Christ, but instead solidifies a love for Christ along the way. The book chronicles a series of interviews with experts in a variety of Christian beliefs. Armed with knowledge he acquired from studying the conclusions of the Jesus Seminar, Lee set out on his journey to validate New Testament claims about Jesus.

In the modern view of Christianity, the truth runs contrary to many opinions that seem easier to grasp. The media tends to promote more views in opposition to Christianity than in support of it. Since Lee considered himself part of objective media, it was easier for him to reason that Christians were wrong in their belief than it was to try to understand the truth. One of the compelling bodies of opposition that was getting a lot of media attention was the Jesus Seminar. The Jesus Seminar continues to attempt to dissuade people from believing that Jesus is the Son of God. The Jesus Seminar, which is comprised of 150 scholars and authors, has published a number of writings they claim indicate that the New Testament Jesus was a fake. In their writings, they claim Jesus didn't walk on water, feed the multitudes, change water into wine, or raise Lazarus from the dead. They also claim that Jesus was crucified because he was a nuisance not because he claimed to be the Son of God. Another claim is that the empty tomb is fiction. Lee was going to validate those claims or put them to rest. Lee may not have realized it at the time, but God had His own plan in mind. God was going to use the curiosity of this investigative reporter to turn those assertions upside down. This former atheist was going to be an instrument for God to bring other lost sheep into the fold.

One of Lee's first interviews was with Craig Blomberg, Ph.D., author of *The Historical Reliability of the Gospels,* and professor of New Testament at Denver Seminary. Lee was questioning Dr. Blomberg regarding eyewitness evidence of the resurrection. After sharing all of his evidence, Dr. Blomberg stated,

> You know, it's ironic: The Bible considers it praiseworthy to have a faith that does not require evidence. Remember how Jesus replied to doubting Thomas: 'You believe because you see; blessed are those who have not seen and yet believe.' And I know evidence can never compel or coerce faith. We cannot supplant the role of the Holy Spirit, which is often a concern of Christians when they hear discussions of this kind.
>
> But I'll tell you this: there are plenty of stories of scholars in the New Testament field who have not been Christians, yet through their study of these issues have come to faith in Christ. And there have been countless more scholars, already believers, whose faith has been made stronger, more solid, more grounded, because of the evidence – and that's the category I fall into (p. 52-53)..

Strobel considered himself to be in the first category. He wrote, "...no, not a scholar, but a skeptic, and iconoclast, a hard-nosed reporter on a quest for the truth about this Jesus who said he was the Way and the Truth and the Life" (p. 53). It would take more than one interview to provide Lee Strobel with the evidence he was seeking. While he pondered his next move, the Holy Spirit was at work aligning more resources for Lee to interview.

As Lee continued his investigation he was touched by the devotion and strength of commitment of early Christians who were persecuted, tortured, and executed for their faith in Jesus as Lord. He began to question why they would hold so strongly to their conviction if there wasn't some truth to it.

Lee's investigation eventually led him to Dr. Gregory Boyd, professor of theology at Bethel College. Dr. Boyd, pastor at Woodland Hills Church in St. Paul, MN., is the author of *Cynic Sage or Son of God? Recovering the Real Jesus in an Age of Revisionist Replies,* a devastating critique of the Jesus Seminar research of 1996. Dr. Gregory's other credentials include an undergraduate degree from the University of Minnesota, a master of divinity from Yale University, and his doctorate from Princeton Theological Seminary.

Many people who have read the findings of the Jesus Seminar and understand the qualifications of the people involved equate the findings to all scholars. So naturally there is a tendency to believe the findings, especially when the media isn't reporting facts that contradict the Seminar. Lee engaged Dr. Boyd regarding several issues from the Jesus Seminar reports. Lee asserted, "The Jesus Seminar paints itself as being on an unbiased quest for truth, as compared with religiously committed people – people like you – who have a theological agenda" (p. 115). Dr. Boyd replied,

> Their major assumption – which, incidentally, is not the product of unbiased scholarly research – is that the gospels are not even generally reliable. They conclude this at the outset because the gospels include things that seem historically unlikely, like miracles – walking on water, raising the dead. These things, they say, just don't happen. That's naturalism, which says that for every effect in the natural world, there is a natural cause.
>
> They [the Jesus Seminar scholars] operate under the assumption that everything in history has happened according to their own experiences, and since they've never seen the supernatural, they assume miracles have never occurred in history.
> Here's what they do: they rule out the possibility of the supernatural from the beginning, and then they say, "Now bring on the evidence about Jesus." No wonder they get the results they do (p. 116).

No matter what questions Lee posed to Dr. Boyd from the Jesus Seminar findings, the conclusions were always the same - the Jesus of the New Testament is the real thing. Lee wrote, "I had already heard well-supported eyewitness, documentary, corroborating, and scientific evidence supporting the New Testament claim that he is God incarnate, and I was getting ready to hit the road again to dig out even more historical material about his character and resurrection" (p. 127).

Lee did continue his investigation for several months after the interview with Dr. Boyd. He interviewed many learned scholars on a variety of New Testament claims with the same results. There was no denying that Jesus was not only the Son of God, but was indeed God incarnate. Lee confides,

> Frankly, I had wanted to believe that the deification of Jesus was the result of legendary development in which well-meaning but misguided people slowly turned a wise sage into the mythological Son of God. That seemed safe and reassuring; after all, a roving apocalyptic preacher from the first century could make no demands on me. But while I went into my investigation thinking that this legendary explanation was intuitively obvious, I emerged convinced it was totally without basis.
>
> In light of the convincing facts I had learned during my investigation, in the face of this overwhelming avalanche of evidence in the case for Christ, the great irony was this: it would require much more faith for me to maintain my atheism than to trust in Jesus of Nazareth! (p. 264 – 265).

Lee's decision to trust in Jesus didn't complete his journey to repentance. He writes that the journey was complete when, "…I talked to God in a heartfelt and unedited prayer, admitting and turning from my wrongdoing, and receiving the gift of forgiveness and eternal life through Jesus. I told him that with his help I wanted to follow him and his ways from here on out" (p. 269).

The media isn't the only place where skeptics and cynics reside and it hasn't always been that way. People in the media were looked up to and admired for their character and honesty in reporting. Politicians used to be revered in that way as well. Just as people in the media have become hardened and biased, so have politicians. It has gotten to the point where the public doesn't trust either of those groups. The public has become as hardened and skeptical as those that we see as being hardened and skeptical. Is there a way out? The Way has always been Jesus Christ, but for some He is considered a roadblock or an obstacle, rather than the clear path to fulfillment. One person who found his way out of the darkness is Chuck Colson.

I imagine that about 40% of the population is unaware of the Watergate scandal of the early 1970s and the career-changing effects that scandal had on one of the Nixon administration's dirtiest and trickiest lieutenants – Chuck Colson. Since this is not about Chuck's past and the dirty political tricks he used to promote his candidate regardless of who was trampled on in the process, I won't spend any time there. If you want to know more about Chuck's past I suggest reading his book, *Born Again,* which he started penning while he served a prison term for one of his tricky maneuvers.

The Chuck Colson we know today is an author, speaker, columnist, and founder of Prison Fellowship Ministries. His profile describes the struggles many of us have faced, and may still be facing, in our passionate search for instant gratification in a materialistic world.

Charles W. Colson had been raised in a church-going home so he knew about God, but desired to keep God at a distance. People he associated with in the political arena never talked about their own personal relationship with God so there wasn't much of an opportunity for him to engage in Christian fellowship – if he had even wanted to. That started to change after he left his White House staff position and entered private law practice. The occasion for his initial brush with Christian fellowship came during a visit with Tom Phillips, then the president of Raytheon. Tom's life had recently been transformed through his acceptance of Jesus Christ as his Lord and Savior and he was eager to share that with Chuck, who he knew was beginning to be troubled by the events surrounding the Watergate break-in. Chuck describes the meeting in *Born Again.*

> We had talked for twenty minutes and nothing at all had been said about religion. Yet Tom was different. There was a new compassion in his eyes and a gentleness in his voice. "Uh – Brainerd tells me that you have become very involved in some religious activities," I said at last.
>
> Yes, that's true, Chuck. I have accepted Jesus Christ. I have committed my life to Him and it has been the most marvelous experience of my whole live.
>
> My expression must have revealed my shock. I struggled for safe ground. "Uh, maybe sometime you and I can discuss that, Tom." If I hadn't restrained myself I would have blurted out, *What are you talking about? Jesus Christ lived two thousand years ago, a great moral leader, of course, and doubtless divinely inspired. But why would anyone "accept" Him or "commit one's life" to Him as if He were around today?* (p. 87).

Chuck wasn't ready to discuss a relationship with anyone, especially Jesus Christ, but he writes, "I went back to Washington to struggle with my inner malaise – and Watergate – and Phillips's astonishing words" (p. 87)

Chuck Colson hadn't participated in the Watergate planning or execution process, but since he was close to President Nixon he was an easy target for the politico's who were all too eager to turn the tricky tables on him. The more Chuck tried to demonstrate his innocence through the media, the more the media twisted his words and spun their yarn about his participation and guilt. At one particularly difficult time he reflected on his feeling of emptiness, questioned his past life and his purpose, and what his life was really all about. In his doubts he recalled the meeting some months earlier when Tom Phillips started to share his new life in Christ. Chuck writes,

> The meeting in March with Phillips, meanwhile, had remained vivid in my memory. His warmth,

> his kindness, the serenity of his face, the startling words, "I have accepted Jesus Christ and committed my life." I hadn't understood them, but they had a ring of simple, shameless sincerity. Tom represented everything that Watergate and Washington were not: decency, openness, truth. I thought often of Tom's words during this stormy time; even more often I recalled the expression on his face, something radiant, peaceful, and very real. I envied it, whatever it was.
>
> At the time, I was not sure why I called Tom Phillips to seek another get-together while I was in Boston, but he welcomed the call. We agreed to meet Sunday night, August 12, at his home. I was surprised at how much I looked forward to seeing him again (p. 102).

The second meeting with Tom Phillips was the beginning of Chuck Colson's journey to the Cross. It wasn't an instantaneous transformation nor did Chuck open his heart to Christ without some trepidation and doubt, but nonetheless, the journey was underway.

Although Chuck and Tom had been friends for many years, Chuck wasn't ready to bare his soul. He was very guarded about the turmoil that was going on inside. Instead, he wanted to know more about what had happened to Tom. Tom explained that although he appeared to have it all – money, material possessions, position, loving family – his life was not complete. Tom felt there was an emptiness in his life. He started to fill that hole with Scriptures. The more he read, the more he understood that he needed to develop a personal relationship with God. Tom said, "It may be hard to understand, but I didn't seem to have anything that mattered. It was all on the surface. All the material things in life are meaningless if a man hasn't discovered what's underneath them" (p. 105). Chuck was feeling an emptiness as well and was eager to learn more about Tom's search for the Answer. Tom continued, "One night I was in New York on business and noticed that Billy Graham was having a Crusade in Madison Square Garden. I went – curious, I guess –

hoping maybe I'd find some answers. What Graham said that night put it all into place for me, I saw what was missing, the personal relationship with Jesus Christ, the fact that I hadn't ever asked Him into my life, hadn't turned my life over to Him. So I did it – that very night at the Crusade" (p. 105).

Tom's testimony wasn't easy for Chuck to get his arms around. He expressed his struggle as, "To me Jesus had always been an historical figure, but Tom explained that you could hardly invite Him into your life if you didn't believe that He is alive today and that His Spirit is a part of today's scene. I was moved by Tom's story even though I couldn't imagine how such a miraculous change could take place in such a simple way. Yet the excitement in Tom's voice as he described his experience was convincing and Tom was indeed different. More alive" (p. 106).

Chuck tried to rationalize his life to the situations he had been exposed to during his political career. Everything he had done was to promote an agenda that he believed was better for the country than that of the opponent. The world of politics was always dog-eat-dog and he was expected to operate that way if he, or his candidate, was going to win. Winning was what mattered, not how the game was played. The more he shared with Tom, the less he was beginning to believe his own words. He was trying to excuse his way through a life without Christ instead of confronting his real need for Christ in his life. He started to wonder if there could be a better way for him. He states, "Tom believed so, anyway. He was so gentle I couldn't resent what he said as he cut right through it all: 'Chuck, I hate to say this, but you guys brought it on yourselves. If you had put your faith in God, and if your cause was just, He would have guided you. And His help would have been a thousand times more powerful than all your phony ads and shady schemes put together'" (p. 107). Tom shared some words from *Mere Christianity,* by C. S. Lewis. He told Chuck that pride was what was blocking his view of Christ. He read,

> For Pride is spiritual cancer: it eats up the very possibility of love or contentment, or even common sense (p. 109).

With that realization, things began to become clear for Chuck, but he wasn't ready to make the leap of faith quite yet. Tom asked if they could pray together. That was an uncomfortable request for Chuck, but he relented and allowed Tom to pray, although he couldn't muster a prayer of his own.

The meeting, the honesty of Tom's testimony, Tom's willingness to witness to, and pray for his friend, proved more than Chuck's emotional being could withstand. As Chuck started to leave, he had second thoughts about praying with Tom. He started to return to the house when he noticed lights going out and Tom and his wife heading for bed. Chuck pulled away from the house, but couldn't navigate through the tears that began to flow once the effects of the evening took hold. He pulled off the road and took his first step in turning his life over to Christ. Chuck shares,

> With my face cupped in my hands, head leaning forward against the wheel, I forgot about machismo, about pretenses, about fears of being weak. And as I did, I began to experience a wonderful feeling of being released. Then came the strange sensation that water was not only running down my cheeks, but surging through my whole body as well, cleansing and cooling as it went. They weren't tears of sadness and remorse, nor of joy – but somehow, tears of relief.
>
> And then I prayed by first real prayer. "God, I don't know how to find You, but I'm going to try! I'm not much the way I am now, but somehow I want to give myself to You." I didn't know how to say more, so I repeated over and over the words: *Take me.*
>
> I had not "accepted" Christ – I still didn't know who He was. My mind told me it was important to find that our first, to be sure that I knew what I was doing, that I meant it and would stay with it. Only, that night, something inside me was urging me to surrender – to what or to whom I did not know.

> I stayed there in the car, wet-eyed, praying, thinking, for perhaps half an hour, perhaps longer, alone in the quiet of the dark night. Yet for the first time in my life I was not alone at all (p. 112 – 113).

A lot of events took place following that initial step. Chuck found that he wasn't the only Christian in the world of decadence known as Washington, DC. As word of his conversion became known, many of his former adversaries came forward to offer their Christian fellowship, prayers, and support as he dealt with the Watergate scandal and subsequent judgment. God had forgiven Chuck, but he didn't consider his conversion complete until he faced the people he had wronged and asked for their forgiveness. One of the victims of his dirty tricks was Arthur Burns and his wife Helen. After confessing what he had done, Chuck said, "And so Arthur, that is the unhappy story. I can't justify it, and I can never undo the harm it caused, but I thought I owed you this apology. I am very, very sorry" (p. 187). After some discussion the two men prayed together and asked for God's peace and grace on their relationship and their individual journey with Him.

There is a saying, "the bigger they are, the harder they fall." I don't know who came up with those words of wisdom, but they were certainly true in the Watergate scandal. They have also been true in other arenas – like the boxing arena for example. One person who experienced a hard fall was George Foreman. He fell so hard that he had to get help from God to get up.

George's encounter with God was exactly that – an encounter. George was one of *the* best heavyweight boxers of all time. No one seemed to be able to knock him down, until he met Mohammad Ali. About the time Chuck Colson was getting beat up over the Watergate scandal, Mohammad Ali was beating up on George Foreman in Africa. George wasn't going to take that loss lying down though. He picked himself up, dusted himself off, and got back in the race for the coveted heavyweight championship. On his way back to the top, he lost another bout, this time with an opponent that he should have easily beaten.

The year was 1977. The fight was with Jimmy Young. The place was Puerto Rico. Foreman and Young battled back and forth in the 12-round match with Foreman getting knocked down in the final round to clinch the fight for Young. Foreman became quite ill from exhaustion and heat stroke. Foreman believed he had a near death experience as he languished in the dressing room that night. In an October 2007 *Guidepost* article, George says, "...I was taken out of my body. I met God, and realized the life I'd been living without him had been empty" (p. 37).

He believes that God can turn any loss into a gain. His example of that belief is the instance of his loss to Muhammad Ali. Foreman and Ali were more than mere opponents in the ring. Foreman considered them to be enemies. In the article, Foreman states, "After he defeated me in that fight in Africa, I spent months thinking of nothing else but how I'd pay him back. But believe it or not, that defeat turned out to be a blessing" (p. 37). After the encounter with God, he called Ali to tell him about his experience. He wrote, "I told him I didn't hate him anymore. In fact, I told him I loved him! He responded to my kindness, and a true friendship developed between us" (p. 37).

George Foreman loved Ali because God loved him and he loved God. Just because George loved others as he loved himself didn't make his problems go away. He reported that,

> Not too long after I gave my life to the Lord, my first marriage broke up. My then-wife just couldn't cope with the new George she suddenly found herself living with. The pain of her leaving me was so great. And there I was, the pastor of a church. I was supposed to be giving people advice on how to live their lives, when I could barely get my tears to stop long enough to deliver any sermon at all. The pain was so fierce I made a deal with God. *Lord,* I said, *if you'll take away this pain, I promise I'll tell people they can make it through anything* (p. 38).

Well, the next day George woke up feeling dramatically different. There was strength inside of him that hadn't been there before. George is still pastor of a church in Houston sharing his love, and His love, with everyone who will listen to that message of hope.

There is something I noted as I researched this chapter that I want to share with you. When we repent and turn away from our sins, God is gracious and will forgive us those sins. However, we should still confront those who we may have harmed by our sinful ways and seek their forgiveness as well. The Bible doesn't specifically state that requirement, but I found a passage that indicated to me that just seeking forgiveness in one direction isn't enough, especially if we leave God out of the equation. The passage is from Matthew chapter 27. It is the story of Judas changing his mind about betraying Jesus and repenting to the chief priests and elders. The English Standard Version reads,

> Then when Judas, his betrayer, saw that Jesus was condemned, he changed his mind and brought back the thirty pieces of silver to the chief priests and elders, saying, "I have sinned by betraying innocent blood." They said, "What is that to us? See to it yourself." And throwing down the pieces of silver into the temple, he departed, and he went and hanged himself.

Judas might have repented, but he repented to the wrong people. He went to his death without repenting to Jesus, the only One who can cleanse us from our sins and wrongs.

Time of Reflection

Read Matthew 3:2, 4:17, 27:3-10; Ezekiel 14:6, and 18:30-32; Luke 15

- What is your understanding of the requirement for repentance and turning from our sins to righteousness? Should seeking forgiveness from those harmed be part of repentance? Discuss what Jesus says about repentance.
- The prophets were continually calling for the Israelites to repent. What was missing in Israel's repentance?

- Ezekiel called for the Israelites to turn from their idols and renounce their detestable practices as part of their repentance. What are the idols and detestable practices that we cling to today?
- Matthew uses the phrase, "Repent, for the kingdom of heaven is near" 33 times. He quotes John the Baptist as saying it and Jesus as well. Since Jesus had already ascended by the time of his writing, why is he so emphatic that the kingdom is near? Is the kingdom of heaven any nearer today than it was then? Discuss your reasoning.

Inspire Others

> We continually remember before our God and Father
> Your work produced by faith, your labor prompted by love,
> And your endurance inspired by hope in our Lord Jesus Christ
> - 1 Thessalonians 1:3 (NIV)

This is my fun chapter – not that the others weren't - where I get to profile a few of my own, personal heroes, at least those that have passed my new scrutiny. I was both surprised and disappointed with the life of some of the people I had held in high regard. I'm glad that the Holy Spirit has enabled me to align myself with an understanding of God's will through a better understanding of the attributes of a Christ-centered life.

Part of my motivation for writing this book came from a song I heard for the first time in the fall of 2009. It's an old song, but the theme is timeless. The song is titled, <u>Where Have all the Heroes Gone</u> by Bill Anderson. Part of the song goes,

> Where have all our heroes gone? What's come over our great land?
> America is still my home sweet home, but where have all our heroes gone?
> I saw a group of boys the other day standing in the corner of a playground
> looking and laughin' at a magazine.
> I overheard one of the boys say, "Man is he ever cool,"
> and he pointed to the man whose picture was on the magazine cover.
> And everybody kinda said under their breath, "Yeah, he's cool alright."
> And I got sick to my stomach
> because I'd seen the cover and the man that they were talking about.
> He had instigated a riot in one of our major cities last summer,
> and the magazine was writing about how the police were unkind to him,
> the judges were not fair with him,
> And how he talked back and slung his long hair about and cussed
> and did his "thing" and they made him into a regular hero…

> This country needs a lotta things today friends,
> but it doesn't need any one thing anymore than it needs some real heroes.
> Men who know what it means to be looked up to by a grimy faced kid.
> Men who wanna sign autograph books and not deal under the table.
> Men who are willing to play the game with the people who made them heroes.
> Men who don't mind putting on a white hat and saying thank you and please.
> I wish I knew more men that I'd be proud of for my son to look up to and say,
> "Daddy, when I grow up I want to be just like him."

I couldn't get the truth of those words out of my mind. Unfortunately, many of our young people have been taught that success equates to the level of notoriety a person receives for getting into trouble, or how large a contract a professional athlete receives, or how cool a car a person has, or the sex-riddled, vulgar movie an actor made, or any number of secular, materialistic labels we put on people and their so-called success. People of all ages want to have the fame and fortune that someone else has acquired, regardless of how they acquired it.

People have been led astray by idols of all sorts since God made His covenant with the Israelites. The Israelites were drawn away from their covenant with God by false prophets and other self-seeking members of God's chosen people who were not embracing the attributes described in this book or the Commandments from God. The 16th chapter of Ezekiel describes how God selected Jerusalem to be apart from all other nations; how she had been admired and revered by other nations because she followed God's commands. Then she became conceited and sold herself into prostitution and lost her way. Ezekiel prophesied against unfaithful Jerusalem saying, "You not only walked in their [Samaria and Sodom] ways and copied their detestable practices, but in all your ways you soon became more depraved than they…Yet I will remember the covenant I made with you in the days of your youth, and I will establish an everlasting covenant with you" (Ezekiel

16:47,60 NIV). Like Jerusalem we can inspire others and be inspired by others to follow Christ, or we can inspire others and be inspired by others to follow Satan. The people profiled in this chapter chose the former and they have all been an inspiration to me. I hope they will be an inspiration to you as well.

I grew up in a time when television was not the norm. Television screens of my day were about 9" wide and set in the frame of a floor-model radio cabinet. The term "gathering around the television" was exactly that. If you wanted to see the fuzzy figures on the screen you had to get close. Entertainers were truly entertaining and programs were suitable for every member of the family. Profanity of any kind was not tolerated and we lived in a G-rated society – not just "G" for general audience, but "G" for godly.

There were so many inspiring radio and television entertainers in those days that it's hard to single out one to profile. One of the earliest to invoke God's blessing on the audience, before the term "God bless" became passé, was Richard Bernard (Red) Skelton (1913 – 1997). Red closed all of his shows with, "Good night and God bless," and you knew he really meant it. Red could do more to entertain people with few props than anyone I know. All he needed was a hat, a coat, and his hair. Red's hair could be tossed into any configuration and then slicked back with a few strokes of a comb. His fedora could be crumpled into any shape that would lend character to his character. Red's kind of entertainment doesn't seem to get people excited anymore and that's a shame.

Red Skelton inspired others through his humor, his humility, his philanthropy, his compassion, his art, and in many other ways. Red encouraged children to learn to love America as much as he did. He served his country during World War II and swore to protect us, our land, our way of life and our flag. He was very proud of our flag and one of his favorite stories was an explanation of the meaning of the Pledge of Allegiance to our flag. The following narrative was delivered by Red Skelton in 1969. It was supposedly a story from his childhood from about 1923. The story is very poignant since, five years after his death, the final part came under fire by liberals who felt we should strip "under God" from the pledge. As you probably know, "under God" was added in 1954 so Red's rendition of the 1923 Pledge of Allegiance is missing those two words. To hear Red tell the story himself, go to http://www.poofcat.com/july.html. Playing the role of one of his grade school teachers, Red tells this story.

> I've have been listening to you boys and girls recite the Pledge of Allegiance all semester and it seems as though it is becoming monotonous to you. If I may, may I recite it and try to explain to you the meaning of each word?
>
> *I*
> me, an individual, a committee of one.
> *Pledge*
> dedicate all of my worldly goods to give without self pity.
> *Allegiance*
> my love and my devotion.
> *To the flag*
> our standard, Old Glory, a symbol of freedom. Wherever she waves, there is respect because your loyalty has given her a dignity that shouts freedom is everybody's job.
> *Of the United*
> that means that we have all come together.
> *States*
> individual communities that have united into 48 great states. Forty-eight individual communities with pride and dignity and purpose; all divided with imaginary boundaries, yet united to a common purpose, and that's love for country.
> *And to the republic*
> a state in which sovereign power is invested in representatives chosen by the people to govern. And government is the people, and it's from the people to the leaders, not from the leaders to the people.
> *For which it stands, one nation*
> one nation, meaning, "so blessed by God."
> *Indivisible*
> incapable of being divided.
> *With liberty*

132

which is freedom - the right of power to live one's own life without threats, fear, or some sort of retaliation.

And Justice
the principle or quality of dealing fairly with others.

For all
for all, which means, boys and girls, it's as much your country as it is mine.

Since I was a small boy, two states have been added to our country, and two words have been added to the Pledge of Allegiance "under God." Wouldn't it be a pity if someone said that is a prayer and that would be eliminated from schools, too?

It seems we get closer to having no room for God outside of our home or church with each passing generation. Where have we gone wrong? Are we not inspiring young people to seek God? Have we become so independent that we are no longer dependent on Him? Fortunately, we still have some heroes around us who cling to the attributes that reflect a Christ-centered life. Seek them out. Hold them up as examples of how a person can be all he or she strives to be and live a Christian life, too. Red Skelton tried to follow that model in his programs by featuring people who shared his values regardless of network objections.

Following Christ may be more of a challenge for celebrities than for us common folks. At least that's the perception I get from outside the celebrity arena, but they deal with the same issues we do and sometimes those issues bring them into a closer relationship with the Lord. An example of dealing with the pressure of celebrity status while retaining the ability to continue to follow God through good times and trying times is Mr. T. Born, Laurence Tureaud, Mr. T was raised in a Christian home so his core values were rooted and nurtured by his environment. God has provided Mr. T with many opportunities to use his gifts, talents, and position to help others. The more T does for others, the more God does for him. He feels truly blessed.

Mr. T goes about a life of caring for, and sharing with, others without the fanfare that some of his peers seek for themselves. His passion is to serve as Christ would serve. He is always focused on being an inspiration to others. He talks about that focus often. The following are excerpts from an interview with staff from beliefnet.com.

> As a Christian you forgive, and you feed the hungry, and clothe the naked, and you visit the sick, and comfort the lonely. If I'm a true follower of my lord and savior Jesus Christ, I got to do the things you're supposed to be doing.
>
> In 1979, before I got famous, there was a contest called the Toughest Bouncer in America...When I started training for the contest I called my pastor, Rev. Henry Hardy of Cosmopolitan Community Church [in Chicago]... I said, "Pastor Hardy, they're having a contest, and when I win this contest I'm going to give you the money, so you can buy food and clothes for less fortunate people in the community." I won two years in a row—it was over $10,000. I didn't have no car then, but I was blessed. So I gave the money freely, and then my blessing came back in the form of "Rocky III."
> After I gave that money to my church, I got the call a month and a half later. They said Sylvester Stallone is going to do "Rocky III," and he's interested in you. Then they sent me the script, and I auditioned, and I got the part. I'd like to think that because I gave freely, it came back to me. Because I was taught that when you give, God will open up the storehouse to the heavens and pour down blessings you won't even have room enough to store. And that's what's been happening ever since. I tell everybody, I get so much because I give so much. I give freely, I give all my time,

give all my money, give all of my soul. I try to motivate people. I try to inspire them.

I am a sinner who has been saved by grace. It's by the grace of God that I'm here. We all have sinned and fallen short on God's glory. I come home and I ask God to forgive me for my sins. Everyday I ask for a new cleansing. I say, "God, let me show kindness to someone, let me give someone hope. Let me be a light at the end of a tunnel for somebody." I tell people, they say I'm a farmer, I plant the seed of hope, plant the seed of inspiration, plant the seed so they can start praying and believing again.

It's hard not to be inspired by that testimony.

Being from a military background I have to admit that a number of people who have been an inspiration to me have been men and women of uniform as well. In particular are Joe Foss, Joshua Chamberlain, Audie Murphy, and Dan Kirchgesler. Since the story of Audie Murphy (1926 – 1971) flows with the above entertainers, I'll profile him first.

My first encounter with Audie took place when I was a young boy in the 1950s through the movie *To Hell and Back.* My recollections of the movie formed the basis for the following biographical sketch of Audie Murphy.

Audie Murphy was arguably the most decorated combat soldier of World War II. He grew up on a sharecropper farm in Texas. When his father deserted the family in 1936, Audie dropped out of school to provide for the financial needs of his mother and ten brothers and sisters. Early in 1941 his mother died, which left the fifteen-year-old responsible for the farm and family. Later that year he put the three youngest siblings in an orphanage until he could make enough of a home to bring the whole family together again. He fulfilled that commitment upon his return from the war.

In June 1942, with the help of his older sister, he was able to convince recruiters that he was 18 instead of 16, and he enlisted in the Army after being turned down by the Marines and paratroopers because he was too small. Rejection by other branches filled him with a determination to be the best infantry soldier in the Army. Doubts by his superiors about his ability to survive on the battlefield required that he fight the system to get assigned to combat duty. The tenacious Texan might have been small in frame, but he was big in spirit. By the end of 1943 he had participated in the invasion of Sicily, the mainland of Italy, and numerous other notable allied offensives. His inspirational leadership style earned the respect and admiration of peers and superiors alike. Audie was promoted through the ranks and by August 1944 he was the senior sergeant of his platoon. Shortly after that he received a battlefield commission to second lieutenant and in January 1945 he was given command of his company.

For me, events in the battle of Holtzwihr (France) were the most inspiring of his military career. Audie had distinguished himself numerous times before this battle, receiving the Distinguished Service Cross (second only to the Medal of Honor), and two Silver Star Medals for heroism. On that day, January 26, after having been wounded several times, he ordered the remaining 19 men from his company to take shelter in a tree line while he mounted a burning tank to hold off an attack by German tanks and infantry. Calling in artillery strikes while firing the tank's machine gun through smoke and flame, he turned the tide of the battle for the allies. Those events earned him the highest military honor, the Medal of Honor, and a place in history (To Hell and Back, 1955).

Audie Murphy was true to his commitment to his family and raised them in a Christian setting as best a teenager could. He inspired friends, neighbors, and family by his kindness, gentleness, and passion to provide for his family. He also inspired his soldiers and was equally inspired by them. Audie inspired me as well. I admired his ability to work through hardship, adversity, and the loss of most of his military buddies while still clinging to his faith in God. His story reminded me of the trials of Job.

Joe Foss (1915 – 2003) was a friend of my father. They grew up together in Sioux Falls, South Dakota. Joe was a few years ahead of my father in school, but to hear my father tell of their relationship you'd think they were the best of buddies, and Joe was a person that everyone in South Dakota wanted to be buddies with. He was admired throughout the state, and what was not to be admired about Joe Foss – he was a World War II fighter ace, recipient of the Medal of Honor, organized the South Dakota Air National Guard, was a military General, Governor of South Dakota, and first Commissioner of the American Football League.

Joe was born and raised on a farm near Sioux Falls. Times were challenging when he was a young man. They didn't have electricity for the farmhouse, farming was hard work, and Joe had to take over all of the duties when his father died in 1933. To make matters worse, the dust storms of the mid 1930s destroyed his crops and stock. Joe was not going to allow himself to be discouraged though. He had a plan and he was going to do whatever it took to see his plan to fruition. He got a job in a service station, went to college, took flying lessons, and then joined the Marine Reserves so he could attend the Naval Aviation program.

Joe Foss is credited as being the "ace of aces" because of his record as a combat pilot. At one point a movie was in the works with John Wayne playing the role of the military hero. However, as a man of integrity and Christian values, Joe turned down the offer when Hollywood moguls tried to spice up the movie with a fictional love story. Foss continually promoted Christian living, supported Campus Crusade for Christ, and programs for disadvantaged children. He was a television personality hosting two programs, an author, and President of the National Rifle Association. It seems there were few associations or organizations (42 in all) that Joe Foss was not actively engaged in. Joe continues to inspire others through the Joe Foss Institute, which is dedicated to promoting patriotism, public service, integrity and an appreciation for America's freedoms. The institute's vision is, "…to promote an informed patriotism, and to be recognized as the national leader in promoting patriotism in schools and organizations" (Joe Foss Institute, 2010).

One of my military heroes goes back to a time and place that none of us can relate to, except in our imagination. That hero is General Joshua Chamberlain (1828 – 1914). He is a hero that most people came to know as a result of the movie *Gettysburg.* General Chamberlain, then Colonel of the 20th Maine, portrayed by Jeff Daniels, was commander of the infamous left flank unit on Little Round Top at the battle of Gettysburg in July 1863. Although the movie was an emotionally stirring introduction to the General, it hardly told the story of the man.

General Chamberlain was a man of great compassion and concern for others. An example of that compassion was demonstrated on Palm Sunday, April 12, 1865. On that day, General Chamberlain was afforded the honor of receiving the arms of the surrendering Confederate army. In the book, *The Passing of the Armies*, (Chamberlain, 1915/1993) General James McPherson describes an event from that day. "As Gordon approached at the head of these men with 'his chin drooped to his breast, down-hearted and dejected in appearance,' Chamberlain gave a brief order, a bugle call rang out, and the Union soldiers shifted their rifles from *order arms* to *carry arms* – the salute of honor. Startled, Gordon looked up, and with sudden realization turned smartly to Chamberlain, dipped his sword in salute, and ordered his own men to *carry arms.* These enemies in many a bitter battle ended the way not with scorn and humiliation but with 'mutual salutation and farewell…honor answering honor.'" (p. xiii). Chamberlain's gesture of respect undoubtedly inspired all those around him – victor and vanquished alike.

Joshua Chamberlain entered Bowdoin College in Brunswick, Maine, in 1848 after teaching himself to read Ancient Greek – one of nine languages he would become proficient in - a college entrance exam requirement at the time. He excelled at his studies, met a number of influential people while a student, became involved in politics, and graduated with honors in 1852. Chamberlain's family expected him to enter the ministry so he studied an additional three years at Bangor Theological Seminary. Instead of pursuing ministry he felt called to teaching and returned to Bowdoin as professor of rhetoric. Inspired by an appetite for learning and a desire to have a positive influence on the student body, Chamberlain would go on to teach every subject in the curriculum except math and science.

Although Chamberlain wasn't schooled in military strategy and tactics, he felt compelled to respond to the call to relieve the slaves from their unrelenting pain and humiliation of bondage. As in every other activity he dedicated himself to, Chamberlain was an inspiration to everyone around him. Rather than accept responsibility for a position that he was ill-prepared for, he turned down the colonelcy of the 20th Maine so he could serve under a more deserving commander and learn the skills he would need to carry him and his future subordinates through the war. There are many inspirational stories from General Chamberlain's war years, but none more so than the defense of Little Round Top.

The 20th Maine was positioned on the left flank of the whole Union army on the battlefield of Gettysburg. They had been rushed into position with little time to prepare for the first assault by a force that greatly outnumbered the 20th. Assault after assault inflicted a great number of casualties on both sides, but the 20th Maine was in desperate straights due to a lack of ammunition and no means of resupply. With ammunition virtually gone, then Colonel Chamberlain assembled his troops and laid out a bold and daring plan that could mean death or capture of the entire unit, loss of the battle, and possible loss of the war. The plan was to fix bayonets and charge down the hill as the enemy executed the next assault. For anyone who has never experienced a combat situation, I can assure you it takes an inspiring leader to convince a group of scared, thirsty, and exhausted soldiers to take on an enemy with unloaded weapons in the hopes of causing them to surrender, but that was exactly what the men of the 20th Maine accomplished.

Chamberlain was wounded several times during the war. On one occasion he was considered too gravely injured to survive and received a battlefield promotion to General for his courage in the battle. The awarding Commanding General didn't expect to have a living Joshua Chamberlain on his staff when he made the promotion. Needless to say, he survived all of his wounds, but suffered from the injuries for the rest of his life. He never let adversity or pain hold him down though. Following the war General Chamberlain served as President of Bowdoin College, was Governor of Maine, and a successful business man.

One-hundred-forty-seven years later General Chamberlain continues to inspire those who engage in a study of his life. I had the opportunity to be in Brunswick, ME in 2006 on a fall color tour and visited General Chamberlain's grave site. I was amazed and impressed with the number of letters and other memorabilia that people left on his headstone. Why people find that to be a soothing outlet I don't know, but, nonetheless he continues to be admired for his courage, integrity, and Christian values.

I didn't get to know Lt. Dan Kirchgesler (1946 – 1969) even though we had more in common than I thought could be possible. We both served in Vietnam, although at different times. We both graduated in 1964, but from different schools. Dan excelled in school and graduated at the top of his class. I was somewhere below the middle. He joined the Army Reserve and received a commission through the ROTC program. I joined the active Army and served as an enlisted man until some years later when I joined the Army National Guard and received my commission. The biggest irony in our lives was the common attraction we shared for a beautiful woman who was a year younger than us. Her name is Carmen. Carmen went to school with me and was my first real love. Unfortunately for me, she went to college, met Dan, and married him instead. I have to say that she made the better choice. It's sad that their life together was too short.

Dan not only excelled in school, but in the military as well. He received the highest honors available in ROTC, and in the active Army Officer Training program. Dan's actions inspired others to excel, especially the people in his company in Vietnam. Dan always volunteered his platoon to take the lead in combat operations. His men were better trained for that role than any other platoon. That's where Dan was when he was killed in action on August 21, 1969 – leading his men. His commander, Gene Shurtz, shared the feelings of all of the members of Dan's unit in a letter to his family after his death. His commander wrote in part, "Daniel was an exemplary officer whose absence from our battalion will be keenly felt by all its members. He was an outstanding officer who was liked and respected by all his associates. His compassion for his men and concern for their welfare endeared each and every soldier to him, making his death a shocking experience for all of us."

After the war his commander communicated with Dan's sister and shared these additional comments about the man he knew,

> He [Dan] was all business…a true professional. He was perhaps the one shining light and my anchor in the storm we were about to encounter. He

> looked tall, tanned, and to-die for blond.... He was a man of few, but powerful words. I immediately knew I could implicitly trust him.... I just knew that no matter what was ahead of us, if Dan were "covering my back," I would be in the best shape possible....
>
> Dan volunteered the 2nd platoon to be point when we were to move out. He had surveyed the situation, a new CO, two new brother platoon leaders, and 17 or so new replacements in the other platoons; all of which had no combat experience. He felt his seasoned platoon would best provide the point security at the time.
>
> ...His platoon had the reputation of being very good at point with success measured in as few casualties as possible. He really was an officer dedicated to bringing as many of his men back as possible (Kennedy and Smithling, 2006).

Even though I didn't get to know Dan, I feel as though I know him as well as I know any member of my own family. I visited Dan at the Vietnam Memorial in Washington, DC. What an emotional reunion that was. I reached up to touch his name and for an instant I felt as though he was there with me. I miss him, but I know we will be together at the table when Christ comes again.

There is one other Vietnam veteran that I would like everyone to get to know. Again, I didn't get to know him personally, but I'm certain we share a life in Christ together. This man was a true Vietnam veteran – he was a villager from Song Be, near the Cambodian border. It was January 1968 and the Tet offensive had just been launched by North Vietnam. Tet was a Vietnamese holiday that had previously been observed by a cease-fire, but that would not be the case in 1968. My unit was stationed near Song Be and our camp, as well as the villages around us, came under attack. When the North Vietnamese swept through a village, they made it a practice to intimidate local village chiefs so they wouldn't support our effort there. In this case, they were going to make an example of the leader of Song Be by executing him. As they led him out for public execution he asked his Father in heaven to, "Forgive them, for they know not what they do." It has been more than forty years since that man gave his life for his country and I still can't shake that testimony from my mind or my heart. His sacrifice has inspired me in more ways than I even know.

When I was growing up in the 1950s and 1960s it was uncommon to find businesses open on Sunday. Most company owners and managers honored God's command to keep holy the Sabbath. Some will argue that the Sabbath is not a particular day of the week like Sunday, but any day that a person chooses to set aside to honor God. That's a more liberal view that didn't exist in the more conservative times that many of us refer to as "the good old days." Fortunately, the good old days still exist in some places. For instance, I have personally taken account of my own Sabbath actions and decided that I will not frequent businesses on Sunday so as not to create demand for a person to work who should be taking advantage of the day to honor God or spend quiet time with family. There is also Lake Benton, Minnesota. Lake Benton is one of many small towns that still practice conservative values. Travelers might find a gas station open on Sunday, but the streets of downtown Lake Benton are quiet on Sunday. What a wonderful feeling to be able to share that peace in the materialistic world of today. There is also another island of peace that many cities share in common; that island is the fast-food restaurant – Chick-fil-A.

There are at least 1000 Chick-fil-A restaurants in the United States and all of them are closed on Sunday. The founder, Truett Cathy, believes that all of his employees deserve to take Sunday as a time of reflection, worship, relationship development, and regeneration. Chick-fil-A's corporate purpose statement, "To glorify God by being faithful stewards of all that is entrusted to us. To have a positive influence on all who come in contact with Chick-fil-A," should be an inspiring and guiding principle for all businesses and individuals alike. The *Guidepost* October 29, 2008 article "Chain Reaction," states, "'Our bodies and minds need time to recharge," Truett said. "How can I teach the 13-year-old boys in my Sunday school class to observe the Sabbath if my cash registers are jingling in my restaurants?"' (Schneider, 2008).

Jesus said, "My Father will honor the one who serves me" (John 12:26b NIV). Truett and his leadership team discovered how true those words are during the difficult economic times of the 1980s. In the same *Guidepost* article, Truett reflects on those days,

> I felt a lot of emotional strain," Truett says. "I didn't know how high expenses would rise or how low sales would slide. I fought the temptation to raise prices knowing this would reduce our volume." And then there was the ever-increasing pressure to do business on Sundays. The big chains were all open on Sundays, when malls were full of hungry shoppers.
>
> Truett decided that employee pay cuts and layoffs were not an option. So he did what he thought was right: He quit taking a salary himself. The uncertain months rolled on. Truett remembers "spending many days and nights in prayer asking God for guidance."
>
> Heeding Christ's words "Come away by yourselves to a lonely place, and rest a while," Truett scheduled a retreat for his executive committee at a lake outside the city. Away from the bustle of the office, the executives talked freely about their concerns and goals.

One of the outcomes of that retreat was the corporate purpose statement shared above. By trusting in God and continuing to honor the Sabbath, the Chick-fil-A corporation has achieved greater financial success than any of their competitors. Maybe there is a lesson to be learned from the inspiring business model that Truett and his staff reflect.

There's a guy that most people have come to know as a man of great energy, vision, insight, and compassion. He hosts a prime-time, inspirational show on network TV, has his own line of furniture, is spokesperson for many of the products we use and consume, and even has his own magazine. His name is Ty Pennington.

Ty is not ashamed to give God the glory for his success. As a youngster, Ty had so much energy that he was continually getting into trouble in school and created one challenge after another for his mother. He believes that God gave him that excess energy to serve His will and to inspire others through his creative and innovative intellect. Ty could visualize uses for things that others couldn't, and he could turn those visions into reality. In the August 1, 2008 *Guidepost* article titled, "Design for Life," Ty tells of a three-story tree house he built one day when his mother had sent him outside to work off some of his energy. He recounted how late in the day his mother came out to check on him.

> Mom came out to get my thermos and looked up. Her jaw dropped. "Ty, you are something else!" At that moment, I realized that no matter what any teacher said about me, here was something I could do. Something that made me happy and Mom proud. There was a plan for me.
> I held on to that. I wasn't stupid. Mom knew it too. God had given me skills that didn't show up on an SAT exam. By the time I went off to college I was diagnosed with ADHD (attention-deficit/hyperactivity disorder), and properly treated.

I have been a fan of the show, *Extreme Makeover – Home Edition,* for some time. Every show is an emotional journey depicting how we should all be living our life - caring for, and sharing with, each other. I've seen Ty inspired by the people the show helps and I've had the opportunity to hear their inspiring stories. Ty shared why he wanted to be part of the program and why the program means so much to him.

> I wanted people to know that their dreams, the impossible things that they had hoped for, really could come true. The people on our show always amaze me. They lose jobs, they face catastrophic illnesses, but they never give up.

> At the end of the show, when everyone shouts, "Move that bus!" and the family gets to see their dream house for the first time, I ask them to take a private off-camera moment to give thanks.
> We're in the business of making their dreams, their greatest hopes, come true. That's one of the most amazing things you can do for a person, a gift not just from the recipient but for the giver. I never would have guessed that it's what I would do for a living. But then all along I think I've been part of a larger plan (Pennington, 2008).

I believe Ty is an example of the mysterious way God works in our life. Something that was looked upon as a curse – Ty's excess energy and knack for getting into trouble – is being used to inspire, encourage, and give hope to others. Ty knew there was a plan for his life; he just needed to be patient and wait for God to reveal it.

Young people can be easily inspired by people of prominence, especially sports figures. There are a number of wonderful, Christian role models in sports, but there are others who are not. Parents should be involved in the process of modeling behavior, especially if children are aspiring to be like a person who is not exemplifying Christ-like values. Positive role models are people such as Dave Dravecky, and Payne Stewart.

Dave Dravecky hadn't always been the Christ-like role model for young baseball fans. Dave didn't stray far from his Catholic roots, but there was a time when he felt his athletic ability came from his own hard work and he didn't really need God to help him out. In his autobiography, *Comeback,* Dave states,

> I grew up in a devout Catholic home, and I always tried to practice my faith. To me that meant attending church once a week. Sunday morning was the timeslot for respecting God.
> During the baseball season, going to church on Sunday wasn't easy. When I was in the minor leagues I kept going to baseball chapel. Baseball chapel is a brief, voluntary meeting held at the

> ballpark on Sunday before the game. I went so regularly that in Buffalo, New York, I became the chapel leader.
>
> We usually had guest speakers for chapel, and I heard a lot about God from them. Many of them gave testimonies about a personal relationship with God. But that kind of talk didn't really click for me.
> I didn't really need God. I'd always depended on my own abilities and my own drive, and I'd done pretty well with that. I thought of myself as a decent person. God received his due on Sunday morning. The rest of my life belonged to me (p. 67-68).

That may have been how Dave felt, but God's covenant calls us to be more involved than just one hour, once a week. After all, He is watching over us all day, every day as He honors His covenant with us.

A slump in his career combined with his participation in the chapel group – albeit limited and unmotivated - made him reevaluate himself, and his relationship with God. After his release from a contract in Columbia he went home to his wife, Janice, a subtly different person. He wrote, "I was no longer so sure of my ability to make life work in my favor. I'd found some things were beyond my control. I'd called out to God for help, in a sense suggesting – although I could not have put this in words – that perhaps he deserved more than respect one hour a week. My image of him was ripe for change" (p. 72).

After being transferred to a San Diego Padres farm club in Amarillo, Dave met Bryon Ballard. Bryon would introduce Dave to a God that he hadn't known before. Bryon's approach to problem solving was much like President Reagan's. They both promoted the belief that the answers to all of our problems can be found in the Bible. Bryon's approach to fostering Dave's relationship with God didn't come from personal coaching. Instead of giving Dave answers to his questions, he showed him how to find answers in the

Bible. With Bryon's help and encouragement, Dave developed a relationship with God that would strengthen and comfort him as his career continued to unfold.

A lump on Dave's pitching arm deltoid muscle was eventually diagnosed as cancer, which required the removal of most of the muscle. A pitcher without a deltoid muscle is like a Kentucky Derby rider without a horse. But Dave didn't give up. With God's help he was able to overcome all the odds and return to the level of professional play that he had before his surgery. The comeback was an opportunity to give glory to God for the work that He was doing in Dave's and Janice's lives. His comeback drew national attention and gave Dave an opportunity to witness to others and to draw attention to special causes. One particular cause was for a young boy with leukemia. Dave received many letters and pledges of financial support. He shared some of those letters in his book. A couple are worthy of sharing with you again (p. 191).

> Gentlemen:
>
> Please accept the enclosed $100 check as my contribution toward Life-Savers. I was lucky enough to have been at the 'Stick this afternoon and I'm still feeling blown away by the experience. The fact that Dave Dravecky was able to pitch so well after having gone through what he's gone through was amazing in and of itself; but I find I'm even more impressed by the strength of character and inner serenity that he's exhibited throughout his ordeal. He's one of the only people I can think of whom I would describe as truly inspirational, and I feel honored to be able to donate some money in his name toward a cause that he considers worthwhile. I wish I could give a million dollars instead of a hundred.
>
> This hasn't been a great year for role models in baseball, but Dave Dravecky is a happy exception to that rule. I feel proud to be a Giants fan.
> Very truly yours,
> S. P.

Dear KNBR staff,

I want to thank KNBR for accepting money on behalf of Dave Dravecky, and for the integrity with which you are covering his story. You have allowed him to be who he is, to speak about his faith, even though people who do not understand the impact of a genuine faith might scoff or complain about hearing his words.

Who would parents want their son to be like? I certainly know the answer for myself. It is too bad that we make heroes of people who are not heroic in their personal living. No matter how much we may like some of Elvis's music, the world will survive without any of it. It will survive without baseball, and I am a loyal, enthusiastic Giants fan! It will not survive without the moral integrity and faith integrated into life as exhibited by Dave Dravecky. Dave is not perfect, I'm sure; no one on earth is. But he is an inspiration to us all, a true example of a great person, whose life multiplied many times would make our country a far safer and more caring and rewarding place to live!

Appreciatively,
S. G.

Dave's comeback was short lived. On August 15, 1989, Dave Dravecky threw a pitch that was heard around the world. Crumbling to the ground with a broken pitching arm, Dave's career was over, but his ability to inspire others wasn't. He received many letters of encouragement after that incident. One was especially poignant (p. 211).

Dear Dave and Janice,

I am a single parent and my son has not seen his dad in four years. In February he started Little League here in Foster City. From that first practice he loved the game.

Dave, when you shared at school my little boy was like a sponge absorbing every word you spoke. The main reason for this note is to say thanks. I know this has been a year of peaks and valleys. In your joys and pain you've given our Lord the glory and you have helped teach my son what a godly man is.

I too have had tough trials in my Christian walk, but God's grace is sufficient. Please know you are in our prayers. I know you must have many people in your life, pulling in all directions. I just wanted to thank you for making a difference in my son's little life. Thanks too for making your life an open window so little boys all over this country can see Jesus in a man they admire and respect.
In Him,
K. H.

Another athlete who garnered respect and admiration for the conduct of his life on and off the field is Payne Stewart (1957 – 1999). Seeing Payne in his golfing attire might cause a person to think that he was a pretentious, showy, self-centered man craving media attention, but Payne was really a humble, caring, sharing, family man. It was Payne's flair that got my attention, but it was his walk with Christ that inspired me. Being just a so-so golfer myself, I needed a little flair of my own to spice up the game so I made my own knickers just like Payne and looked the part, even though I couldn't play the part. Catching the attention of other golfers through my attire kept their focus off my game, which was pretty embarrassing.

Tracey Stewart, Payne's wife, chronicled his life in a book simply titled, *Payne Stewart.* She tells the story of Payne's journey to the Cross. She wrote, "Payne never claimed to have a great knowledge of the Bible. Nor did he try to tell anyone else how to live. 'I'm not a Bible thumper,' he said. 'I can't get up there on a rock and tell you what it all means because I don't know. But I'm learning, and I live what I'm learning" (p. 261). Payne and I are much alike in that regard, and I'm sure there are others who view their journey with Christ as being a work in progress. I don't think I've arrived yet, but I'm learning to love the Lord more every day. Tracey shared a funny story about Payne's biblical learning process.

> Once, for example, Payne was with Chris Millsaps at The First Academy, and someone gave him a card with a Scripture reference that said "I Thess." Payne was touched by the card and the Scripture reference, and said, "Look at that – First Theologians…" Chris didn't have the heart to tell Payne that the book he was referring to was First Thessalonians!
>
> He never pretended to have the answers and probably didn't know what some of the questions were. But his faith was genuine, and as he understood the Bible, the issue wasn't about how much faith he had but whether his faith in Christ was real. And everyone close to Payne knew that his faith was real (p. 261).

Although Payne was uncertain about chapter and verse, he took every opportunity to share his faith with anyone willing to lend an ear, and with those who just happened to be a captive audience at the moment. At a press conference following his 1999 US Open win, Payne had a captive media audience so he took the opportunity to give God the glory for his success that year. Tracey wrote,

> The reporters listened respectfully as Payne talked about his faith in the Lord. "I'm proud of the fact that my faith in God is so much stronger, and I'm so much more at peace with myself than I've ever been in my life," Payne said. "And that's the reason that I was able to gather myself and conduct myself. And where I was with my faith last year and where I am now is leaps and bounds.

> And that gave me the strength to stand up there and believe in myself and get the job done."
> Payne continued to answer questions for nearly an hour, and at the close of the press conference he said, "I'm a lot more mentally prepared to deal with these situations than I have been in the past. I'm going back to the fact that my faith is strong. And the Lord's given me the ability that he wants me to use so I can stand up here and give him the praise" (p. 273).

Later that year, Payne had another opportunity to share his testimony with a captive audience. This time it was at the Legacy Awards dinner. Tracey again shares,

> …Payne was asked to say a few words following the presentation. His voice cracked with emotion as he said, "I think that we all have something in common in that we have dreams. And the thing about dreams is that sometimes you get to live them out. I've always dreamed about playing golf for a living. And here I am living out my dream.
> "It's pretty special. I've accomplished quite a bit in my career, and this year has been extremely special, but really what excites me, probably as much as winning, is being able to make a difference in people's lives."
>
> "It's not that hard to give something back. I've been blessed with an ability; I think God chose me to play golf, and I use that podium; I use the golf course to give him the praise that he deserves and to make a difference in people's lives…so it's not that hard to give a little bit back" (p. 285-286).

Payne touched many lives. Golf is a sport grounded in integrity so there are probably more Christians willing to openly share their testimony than in most other sports. At Payne's funeral, Paul

Azinger shared what Payne's life with Christ was really all about. He said,

> Payne Stewart has finished the race, he has kept the faith, and now the crown of righteousness is his. Payne Stewart loved life and loved people... During this past year, everyone who knew Payne Stewart saw this dramatic change in his life. They saw in Payne what the Bible calls a 'peace which passes all understanding.' Only God can do that because only God can change a heart.
>
> It is an honor to stand before you as Payne Stewart's, Robert Fraley's, and Van Ardan's friend. And because I knew them so well, I know what they would have wanted me to say in my closing remarks. Whoever you are, wherever you are, whatever you have done; if you feel the tug of God's Spirit on your heart, do not turn away. If, like Payne, Robert, and Van, you want to know the happiness and peace that only Jesus Christ can bring, I invite you to confess your sins and receive him as your Savior. Regardless of what your life has brought you, his love is enough. And his peace is for real (p. 307-308).

Among the personal belongings that were retrieved from the plane crash were his wedding ring, college ring, a gold pendant, other personal items, his devotional books, and his WWJD bracelet. Tracey said that as she leafed through the devotional she came across the passages that Payne would have been studying the day of the crash. The passages are (p. 311-312),

> Intercession
> Grant that I may be used to open the eyes of others and to turn them from darkness to light, and from the power of Satan to God, so that they may receive forgiveness of sins, and an inheritance

among those who have been sanctified by faith in Jesus. Acts 26:18

Affirmation

Blessed is the man who perseveres under trial, because when he has been approved, he will receive the crown of life that God has promised to those who love him. James 1:12

Thanksgiving

Bless the Lord, O my soul;
And all that is within me, bless His holy name.
Bless the Lord, O my soul,
And forget not all his benefits;
Who forgives all your iniquities
And heals all your diseases;
Who redeems your life from the pit
And crowns you with love and compassion;
Who satisfies your desires with good things,
So that your youth is renewed like the eagle's.
Psalm 103:1-5

Closing Prayer

The Lord is my rock and my fortress and my deliverer;
My God is my rock; I will take refuge in Him,
My shield and the horn of my salvation,
My stronghold and my refuge –
My savior, You save me from violence.
I call on the Lord, who is worthy of praise,
And I am saved from my enemies 2 Samuel 22:2-4.

Payne Stewart will continue to be an inspiration to me, as I hope he is to all who read this book, but the focus is not on Payne, the focus needs to be on living a life that inspires others to follow your footsteps to the Cross. I'm sure Payne would prefer that.

Time of Reflection

Read the Scripture verses from Payne's devotional again.
- What an inspiring intercession Paul shares with us in Acts 26. It sounds like a simple request. Discuss how challenging it is to live that prayer.
- Discuss the various theological interpretations of sanctification. One definition for sanctification is to be made holy. How can someone be "made holy" while still considering him- or herself as a work-in-progress on the journey with Christ?
- Discuss how you have been inspired by others during your journey to the Cross.
- Are you patiently waiting for God to reveal His plan for your life? What are you doing to prepare for God to use you to fulfill His plan?

Epilogue

As I started researching material for this book I felt challenged to find people to profile who exemplified Christ-like values. I was hampered in my search by my personal bias towards people who I selfishly wanted to fit the search criteria. This may seem contradictory, but when I shed my bias and broadened my search, I became increasingly aware that we have invisible heroes nearer than we realize. It seemed like every person I profiled led me to another person who led me to another person and so on. Many of them I had never heard of before, yet they have been around me all of my life – I just never bothered to seek them out. One person in particular, Jim Elliot, who was profiled in an early chapter, seemed to have an influence on many of the people profiled. Jim's crown is one that links all of the attributes of this book together. I'm glad I got to know him through his work and through the people he influenced. It seems as though Christian birds seem to flock together.

I have become more convinced than ever that the thread that binds all of these people together is their common trust in Jesus' words to His disciples before The Sermon on the Mount. Jesus said,

> Therefore I tell you, do not worry about your life, what you will eat or drink; or about your body, what you will wear. Is not life more important than food, and the body more important than clothes? Look at the birds of the air; they do not sow or reap or store away in barns, and yet your heavenly Father feeds them. Are you not much more valuable than they? Who of you by worrying can add a single hour to his life?
>
> And why do your worry about clothes? See how the lilies of the field grow. They do not labor or spin. Yet I tell you that not even Solomon in all his splendor was dressed like one of these. If that is how God clothes the grass of the field, which is thrown into the fire, will he not much more clothe you, O you of little faith? So do not worry, saying, "What shall we eat?" or "What shall we drink?" or

"What shall we wear?" For the pagans run after all these things, and your heavenly Father knows that you need them. But seek first his kingdom and his righteousness, and all these things will be given to you as well. Therefore do not worry about tomorrow, for tomorrow will worry about itself (Matthew 6: 25-34a NIV).

An unsettling discovery that my research led me to is that there are far more "professing" Christians around me than I realized. I say professing Christians because if there really is a large number of true, Bible-believing Christians in this country, then our nation's leadership should be more reflective of the attributes highlighted in this book. That doesn't seem to be the case. If it were true, we wouldn't be debating homosexual agendas, same-sex marriage, abortion, redistribution of wealth to sluggards, and a reliance on government to be the caregiver to widows and orphans. Jesus spoke out against the moral issues that we openly embrace and he commanded that we, not the central government, take care of the widow and orphans. God said to Jeremiah, "My people have been lost sheep; their shepherds have led them astray and caused them to roam on the mountains" (Jeremiah 50:6a NIV). It may be wrong to lay all of the blame on the shepherds because we are the ones who put the shepherds in their place of leadership and allow them to rule unchecked. Let us pray that our nation doesn't suffer God's wrath as the Israelites did when they ignored their covenant with Him. There is still time for us to turn away from the false shepherds that we are following today and align our path with shepherds that will lead us to the Cross.

I started this book with the words of a song about heroes, and I will close in the same way. However, these words are more uplifting and hopefully reflect where your heart is after reading this book. The song is titled <u>I Want to be Just Like You</u> by Phillips, Craig, and Dean. The song describes the true hero image that we should be displaying to everyone we come in contact with.

> He climbs in my lap for a goodnight hug
> He calls me Dad and I call him Bub

With his faded old pillow and a bear named Pooh
He snuggles up close and says, "I want to be like you"
I tuck him in bed and I kiss him goodnight
Trippin' over the toys as I turn out the light
And I whisper a prayer that someday he'll see
He's got a father in God 'cause he's seen Jesus in me

Lord, I want to be just like You
'Cause he wants to be just like me
I want to be a holy example
For his innocent eyes to see
Help me be a living Bible, Lord
That my little boy can read
I want to be just like You
'Cause he wants to be like me.

Reference List

A pro-life Mother! (2010, January 27). Entry post. Retrieved April 19, 2010, from http://blogs.palmbeachpost.com/gatorbytes/2010/01/27/will-tebows-pro-life-commercial-affect-his-draft-stock-or-marketability/

Albom, M. (2009, October 4). Ernie's Words Still Make a Night Magic. Retrieved April 17, 2010, from http://mitchalbom.com/journalism/article/5807

Anthony, B. (1999, July). A Place for Mike. *Guideposts,* p.26-30.

Associated Press. (2010, January 12). *Miep Gies, who helped Anne Frank, dies.* Retrieved April 18, 2010, from http://www.msnbc.msn.com/id/34814027

Beamer, L., Abraham, K. (2002). Let's Roll. Wheaton, IL: Tyndale House Publishing, Inc.

Bill Gaither. (2010, April 12). In Wikipedia, The Free Encyclopedia. Retrieved April 13, 2010, from http://en.wikipedia.org/wiki/Bill_Gaither_(gospel_singer)

Billy Graham. (2010, April 12). In Wikipedia, The Free Encyclopedia. Retrieved April 13, 2010, from http://en.wikipedia.org/w/index.php?title=Billy_Graham

Boone, P. (1970). A New Song. Carol Stream, IL: Creation House.

Breslau, K., Clift, E., Thomas, E. (2001, November 26). *The Real Story of Flight 93.* Retrieved April 15, 2010, from http://www.papillonsartpalace.com/real.htm

Brockway, L. S. (2010). *Interview with Zach Bonner.* Retrieved April 11, 2010, from http://www.beliefnet.com/Inspiration/2009/12/Interview-with-Zach-Bonner.aspx

Callopy, M. (1996). Works of Love and Works of Peace (Online). Available: http://www.ewtn.com/motherteresa/words.htm

Caring Institute (1992). Caring Award. Retrieved April 11, 2010, from http://www.caring-institute.org/caringawards.taf

Carson, B., Murphey, C. (1990). Gifted Hands - The Ben Carson Story. Grand Rapids: Zondervan

Chamberlain, J. (1993). *The Passing of the Armies.* New York: Bantam Books. (Original work published 1915)

Character. 2010. In *Merriam-Webster Online Dictionary*. Retrieved April 11, 2010, from http://www.merriam-webster.com/dictionary/character

Colson, C. (1976). Born Again. New York: Spire Publishing

Conor Oberst. (n. d.). Thinkexist.com. Retrieved April 18, 2010, from http://thinkexist.com/quotation/i-came-upon-a-doctor-who-appeared-in-quite-poor/365911.html

Diary of Alvin York (2010). Retrieved April 15, 2010, from http://acacia.pair.com/Acacia.Vignettes/The.Diary.of.Alvin.York.html

Dravecky, D., Stafford, T. (1990). Comeback. Grand Rapids: Zondervan

Ernie Harwell. (2010, March 25). In Wikipedia, The Free Encyclopedia. Retrieved 18:57, April 18, 2010, from http://en.wikipedia.org/w/index.php?title=Ernie_Harwell

Everett, A. (composer), Slade, M. (lyrics). (1871). Footsteps of Jesus (Music). Public Domain

Fidelity. 2010. In *Merriam-Webster Online Dictionary*. Retrieved April 17, 2010, from http://www.merriam-webster.com/dictionary/fidelity

Foreman, G. (2007, October). Ringside Seat. *Guideposts,* p.34-38.

George Washington Carver. (2010, April 10). In Wikipedia, The Free Encyclopedia. Retrieved April 11, 2010, from http://en.wikipedia.org/wiki/George_Washington_Carver

George Washington Carver. (n.d.). BrainyQuote.com. Retrieved April 13, 2010, from http://www.brainyquote.com/quotes/authors/g/george_washington_carver.html

Graham, B. (1997). Just as I am. New York: HarperCollins.

Griffiths, L. (2007, February 3). No Arms, no legs, no worries for evangelist. *East Valley Tribune* [online], Retrieved April 13, 2010 from http://www.religionnewsblog.com/17383/nick-vujicic

Halamandaris, B. (1999). Be The Light - a blueprint for a happy and successful life. Marietta, GA: Longstreet, Inc.

Hibbs, J. (Director). (1955). *To Hell and Back* [Motion picture]. Perf. Audie Murphy, Charles Drake, Jack Kelly, David Janssen. Autobiography by Audie Murphy. Universal

International Studios.
Hilley, J. (2008). <u>Sarah Palin - A New Kind of Leader</u>. Grand Rapids: Zondervan.
Huckabee, M. (2008). <u>Do The Right Thing.</u> New York: Sentinel.
Integrity. 2010. In *Merriam-Webster Online Dictionary*. Retrieved April 11, 2010, from http://www.merriam-webster.com/dictionary/integrity
Jacobs, J. (2005). Peacemaker Hero - Craig Kielburger. Retrieved April 18, 2010, from http://myhero.com/go/hero.asp?hero=c_Kielburger
Jamie Kennedy, Angel Smithling. (2006, March 28). Entry post. Retrieved April 21, 2010, from www.vvmf.org
Joe Foss Institute. (2010). Joe Foss Bio. Retrieved April 21, 2010, from http://www.joefoss.com/
John Adams. (n.d.). Brainy Quote.com. Retrieved April 17, 2010, from http://www.brainyquote.com/quotes/authors/j/john_adams.html
Kendrick, A. (Director). (2008). *Fireproof* [Motion picture]. Perf. Kirk Cameron, Erin Bethea, Ken Bevel. Screenplay by Alex and Stephen Kendrick. Sherwood Pictures. US.: DVD (2008).
Kuarlt, C. (Reporter). (1996). *Charles Kuralt's Christmas* (cassette). New York: Simon ad Schuster audio.
Linda Fuller - co-founder of Habitat for Humanity International. (2010). Retrieved April 19, 2010, from http://www.habitat.org/how/linda.aspx
Martin, D. (2009, February 3). Millard Fuller, 74, Who Founded Habitat for Humanity, Is Dead. *New York Times,* p.A28.
Matthews, D. (M.D.). (1999, July). The Healing Effect. *Guideposts,* p.32-33.
McCain, J., Salter, M. (1999). <u>Faith Of My Fathers</u>. New York: Random House.
Millard Fuller - Habitat for Humanity International Founder. (2010). Retrieved April 19, 2010, from http://www.habitat.org/how/millard.aspx
Mr. T. (2010). Interview with Mr. T. Retrieved April 21, 2010, from http://www.beliefnet.com

Pennington, T. (2008, August 1). Design for Life. *Guideposts* [online], p.1-3. Retrieved April 21, 2010, from http://www.guideposts.com/story/design-life

Peterson, R. (1995). Robert Chapman. Neptune, NJ: Loizeaux Brothers, Inc.

philanthropy. 2010. In *Merriam-Webster Online Dictionary*. Retrieved April 11, 2010, from http://www.merriam-webster.com/dictionary/philanthropy

Qualye, D. (1994). Standing Firm. New York: HarperCollins.

Red Skelton - Pledge of Allegiance. (1969). Retrieved April 21, 2010, from http://www.poofcat.com/july.html.

Redistribution Center, Inc. (1991). About Us. Retrieved April 11, 2010. from www.redistributioncenter.org/about.html

Rick Warren, (2008). What Makes a Great President? Retrieved April 17, 2010, from http://www.lhj.com/style/covers/what-makes-a-great-president/

Ronald Reagan (1981). *Inaugural Address.* Retrieved April 17, 2010, from http://www.reagan.utexas.edu/archives/speeches/1981/12081a.htm

Ronald Reagan (1983). *Remarks at the Annual Convention of the National Religious Broadcasters.* Retrieved April 17, 2010, from http://www.reagan.utexas.edu/search/speeches/speech_srch.html

Ronald Reagan (1984). *Remarks at a Dallas Ecumenical Prayer Breakfast,* Retrieved April 17, 2010, from http://www.americanrhetoric.com/speeches/ronaldreaganecumenicalprayer.htm

Ronald Reagan (1989). *Farewell Address to the Nation.* Retrieved April 17, 2010, from http://www.reagan.utexas.edu/archives/speeches/1989/011189i.htm

Rue, G. (2009, November 9). To Whom Much is Given. *Guideposts* [online], p.1-3. Retrieved April 19, 2010, from http://www.guideposts.com/story/sandra-bullock-blind-side-football

Saint, S. (1996, reprinted 2003, July 1), Retrieved April 17, 2010, from http://www.atanycost.org/images/DidTheyHaveToDie.pdf

Samuel Adams, (n.d.). Revolutionary War and Beyond. Retrieved April 17, 2010, from http://www.revolutionary-war-and-beyond.com/samuel-adams-quotes-2.html

Sarah Palin - The Untold Story - In Her Own Word!, (2009), New York: International Merchandising Corp.

Schneider, R. (2008, October 29). Chain Reaction. *Guideposts* [online], p.1-2. Retrieved April 21, 2010, from http://www.guideposts.com/story/positive+thinkers-career-fastfood?

Sheen, F. J. Archbishop. (2010). *Fulton Sheen Biography and Inspiration.* Retrieved April 13, 2010, from http://www.archbishopsheencause.org/fulton-sheen-biography-and-inspiration

Stewart, T., Abraham, K. (2000). Payne Stewart. Nashville: Broadman and Holman Publishers

Strobel, L. (1998). The Case for Christ - A Journalist's Personal Investigation of the Evidence for Jesus. Grand Rapids: Zondervan

Swanson, D. (1997). *John Fling.* Retrieved April 11, 2010, from http://www.swansonphotography.com/photos/caregivers/flinghomepage.html

The Holy Bible. English Standard Version. Wheaton, IL: Good News Publishers, 2007

The NIV Study Bible. 10th Anniversary ed. Grand Rapids: Zondervan, 1995.

Virtual Wall. Sijan. (2006, November 14). Retrieved April 17, 2010, from http://www.virtualwall.org/ds/SijanLP01a.htm

Volin, B. (2010). *Will Tebow's Pro-Life Commercial Affect His Draft Stock or Marketability?* Retrieved April 19, 2010, from http://blogs.palmbeachpost.com/gatorbytes/2010/01/27/will-tebows-pro-life-commercial-affect-his-draft-stock-or-marketability/

Wilkerson, D. (1962). The Cross and the Switchblade. New York: Jove Books

Wonderful!!!!. (2009, May 6). Young People Who Rock. *Ypwr.blog.* Retrieved April 13, 2010, from CNN.http://ypwr.blogs.cnn.com/2009/05/03/zach-bonner/

Zach Bonner. (2010, March 25). In Wikipedia, The Free Encyclopedia. Retrieved April 13, 2010, from http://en.wikipedia.org/w/index.php?title=Zach_Bonner&oldid=351969676

Zig Zigler. (2010). *The Best News*. Retreived April 17, 2010 from http://www.evancarmichael.com/Entrepreneur-Advice/448/The-Best-News.html